GERALD TAN

ASIAN
DEVELOPMENT

An Introduction to Economic, Social and Political Change in Asia

EASTERN UNIVERSITIES PRESS
by Marshall Cavendish

© 2003 Times Media Private Limited

Re-issued 2003
by Times Media Private Limited
(Academic Publishing) under the imprint
Eastern Universities Press
by Marshall Cavendish
First published 2000 under the
imprint Times Academic Press

Times Centre, 1 New Industrial Road,
Singapore 536196
Fax: (65) 6284 9772
E-mail: tap@tpl.com.sg
Online Book Store:
http://www.timesacademic.com

Printed by Vine Graphic Pte Ltd, Singapore
on non-acidic paper

National Library Board (Singapore)
Cataloguing in Publication Data
Tan, Gerald.
Asian Development: An Introduction to Economic,
Social, and Political Change in Asia /
Gerald Tan. – 2nd ed. – Singapore:
Eastern Universities Press, 2003.

p. cm.
ISBN: 981-210-247-7

1. Asia – History – 1945-
2. Asia – Economic conditions.
3. Asia – Politics and government.
4. Asia – Social conditions.
I. Title.

DS35.2
950 — dc21
SLS2003018634

London • New York • Beijing • Shanghai
• Bangkok • Kuala Lumpur • Singapore

Contents

List of Tables

List of Figures

Preface

Important, and far-reaching, changes have taken place in the economic, social and political development of Asian countries (which, in this book, includes South Asia, Southeast Asia and East Asia) since the end of the Second World War. Within the relatively short span of about 50 years, many Asian countries have been transformed from poor, less developed, agrarian countries to affluent, developed, industrial economies. Many have attained important positions in world trade and development. Others are well on their way to similar achievements. In the process of this development, many important social and political changes have occurred in these countries. While these trends are more apparent in some Asian countries than others, all have, to various degrees, experienced the changes that are depicted in this book.

This book presents a systematic introduction to the major trends that have taken place in the economic, social and political development of Asian countries since the end of the Second World War, and explains the factors which account for them. Although it analyses many technical issues, it is written in a manner that is designed to make it accessible to the general reader, who, it is hoped, will be encouraged to continue to study the issues discussed in this book in greater detail.

I wish to thank my many students at Flinders University for providing me with useful comments on parts of this book which I have used in lectures and classes. I also wish to thank my many friends and colleagues, not only in Australia, but also in other parts of the world who have helped me over the years and shared their knowledge with me. Whilst too many to name individually, their generosity and assistance must not go unrecorded. As always, the usual caveat applies. No one but me should be held responsible for any errors or omissions that can often slip by even the most careful pair of eyes.

My wife of many years, Stella, deserves my greatest appreciation and gratitude. She has borne all the burdens of being wife, mother, guardian angel, and soul mate with quiet fortitude, and has asked for nothing in return. Without her unfailing love and support, I would still be struggling to finish my first book, instead of putting the finishing touches to my twelfth.

Gerald Tan
Adelaide
June 2003

1

Introduction

A number of important trends can be discerned in the economic, social, and political development of Asian countries since the end of the Second World War. The term "Asian countries" is used in this book to include the countries of South Asia (Bangladesh, India, Pakistan and Sri Lanka), Southeast Asia (Brunei Darussalam, Indonesia, Malaysia, Myanmar, Philippines, Thailand, Singapore), the former Indo-Chinese states (Cambodia, Laos, Vietnam), and the countries of East Asia (China, including Hong Kong SAR, South Korea and Taiwan). This book identifies and explains these trends, and examines the factors which have led to their emergence. In doing so, it attempts to provide an understanding of the major economic, social and political changes that have taken place in the countries of South, Southeast, and East Asia during the fifty years since the end of the Second World War.

Part I deals with the main trends in the economic development of Asian countries. Chapter 2 examines the colonial heritage of Asian countries, and discusses the ways in which the metropolitan powers developed their colonies, and prepared them for subsequent economic development. Chapter 3 explains the major economic changes that have characterised most Asian countries since the end of the Second World War. These include the shift from agricultural to industrial economies, the introduction, and impact, of new technology in agriculture, the change from import-substituting industrialisation to export-oriented industrialisation, and the move from centralised to market-oriented economies. Chapter 4 contains an analysis of the experience of rapid economic growth in the post-war period, the significant improvements in living standards, and the environmental consequences of rapid industrialisation. Chapter 5 discusses global links and the growing integration of Asian countries in the world economy, the importance of many Asian countries in world development and trade, and the impact of globalisation (including the outbreak of the Asian currency crisis and its consequences), on the economies of Asia.

Not all countries in Asia have experienced these changes to the same extent or degree. In general, these changes are most pronounced in the Newly Industrialising Countries of Asia (Hong Kong SAR, Singapore, South Korea and Taiwan), and least pronounced in the countries of South Asia and the former Indo-Chinese states (with the other countries occupying intermediate positions). Some Asian countries have progressed to such a state that they are now regarded as affluent, developed countries. Others are still at the opposite end of the development spectrum. The reasons for these differences are examined in this book.

Part II examines the major social changes that have been important in Asia. Demographic changes arising from declining fertility are examined in Chapter 6. The expansion, and impact, of increasing educational opportunities (especially for women) are discussed in Chapter 7, while changes in the role and status of women, and of the family unit as well as patterns of marriage and divorce are discussed in Chapter 8. As in the case of economic trends, some Asian countries have experienced tremendous changes in their social fabric over the past fifty years, while others have remained virtually stagnant.

Part III discusses the major trends in the political development of Asian countries. These include the struggle for independence, the rise of Communist regimes, and the emergence of Communist insurgencies in many Asian countries, which are discussed in Chapter 9. The rise of authoritarian states in the post-war period and their importance in the process of economic growth and development are discussed in Chapter 10. The trend towards democratisation toward the end of the 20th century and the factors which explain this are analysed in Chapter 11. Chapter 12 discusses the war on terror and its impacts on Asian countries.

This book is intended as an introduction to the major trends that have taken place in the economic, social and political development of Asian countries. It is written in a manner that is accessible to the general reader, who, it is hoped, will be stimulated to continue to pursue the issues covered in this book in greater detail, long after this book has been read.

PART 1

Economic Transformation

CHAPTER 2

The Colonial Heritage

INTRODUCTION

By the beginning of the twentieth century, most of the countries of Southeast and East Asia had either been colonised by Western imperial powers, or subjugated by them. Only Japan and Thailand escaped this fate. The Japanese colonised Taiwan and South Korea after defeating China in the Sino-Japanese War (1894–95). The defeat of the Japanese in the Second World War saw these territories come under the control of the Americans. The British colonised India, Malaya, Singapore, North Borneo and Sarawak. The Dutch colonised Indonesia, while the French colonised Indochina. The Spanish colonised the Philippines, which later came under the control of the Americans.

By the second half of the twentieth century, the Western imperial powers withdrew from the region, either voluntarily (often as a consequence of a weakening domestic economy), or as a result of their defeat in wars of independence. They left behind indelible marks of their presence, which in many cases, spanned centuries.

Some countries in Southeast and East Asia benefited from their colonial heritage in the form of investments in social infrastructure that their former colonial masters left behind. This was to stand them in good stead in later years. Others were not so lucky, and still bear the scars of their colonial past to this day. All suffered from the humiliation of being ruled (in some cases, very harshly) by foreigners, many of whom were not particularly able, well-educated, cultured, or sophisticated, compared either to the people over whom they lorded, or to their compatriots in the metropolitan centres. It was not uncommon in the 1950s to find police sergeants who had little prospects of promotion in Manchester or Sheffield, arriving in Hong Kong or Singapore as inspectors.

JAPANESE COLONIALISM

In 1894, war broke out between China and Japan over control of the Korean peninsula. Japan regarded Korea as important to its security, as whoever controlled the Korean peninsula could threaten Japan. Both countries had long affiliations with Korea, and claimed sovereignty over it. The modern Japanese navy and army were no match for the ill-equipped and poorly-trained Chinese, who were soon defeated. The Treaty of Shimonoseki (1895), which marked the end of the Sino-Japanese War, ceded Taiwan (then known as Formosa), as well as other territories to Japan. China was forced to renounce its claims over Korea and to recognise its "independence". The latter proved to be short-lived, as the Japanese annexed Korea in 1910. Thus began a long period of Japanese rule over these territories, which ended with Japan's defeat in the Second World War in 1945, when South Korea and Taiwan came briefly under the control of the Americans. Following the Korean War (1950–53), South Korea became an independent country. The status of Taiwan remains unresolved as China still regards it as one of its provinces.

Attempts at modern economic development had already begun in Korea and Taiwan before they came under Japanese control. In Taiwan, a modernisation programme was initiated after it became a separate province of China in 1885. In Korea, a banking system was established between 1897 and 1905, and mining, manufacturing and electricity companies were also established (often, by the Japanese). Once these two territories came under Japanese control, economic development was accelerated. This laid the foundations for rapid economic growth and development after the Second World War.

Apart from security concerns (Korea was like a dagger pointing at the heart of Japan, whilst control of Taiwan would confer command over the sea approaches to the Japanese islands) (Crowley 1976: 225–

230), the Japanese were also interested in Korea and Taiwan as sources of food (especially rice) and raw materials. Lacking in land and natural resources, Japan saw imports of food and raw materials from these two colonies as a means of reducing its large trade deficits.

This led the Japanese to reform and modernise agriculture in Korea and Taiwan. Both territories were already rice producers, and Taiwan already had good irrigation facilities. The Japanese introduced better farming practices and new, high-yielding strains of rice in order to boost productivity (Grabowski 1998: 53–68). In addition, the colonial government invested heavily in infrastructure, building irrigation facilities, roads, power stations, and railways. The Japanese system of education and government administration was also introduced in a bid to assimilate the Koreans and Taiwanese into Japanese culture (Ho 1984: 347–98). Koreans and Taiwanese were not allowed to speak their own languages or wear their traditional attire. Instead, all had to speak Japanese and wear kimonos.

The strategic positions of Korea and Taiwan also led the Japanese to develop industry, especially during the decades prior to the outbreak of the Second World War. Heavy industry (especially steel) was established in North Korea (which was rich in industrial raw materials), while medium and light industries (for example sugar refining and textiles) were established in Taiwan. These paved the way for future economic growth and development (Ho 1975).

Although the Japanese colonial administration was harsh on the local populations (Halliday and McCormack 1973: 146–147), it did develop the economies of Korea and Taiwan. Unlike other colonial powers, the Japanese did not establish enclave plantation agriculture, and it did reinvest profits from industrial development in its colonies. In this sense, both Korea and Taiwan benefited from Japanese colonialism in spite of their populations being very poorly treated by the Japanese. Korea and Taiwan emerged from their colonial period with a relatively healthy and modernised agricultural sector, an industrial base, good infrastructure, a well-educated labour force, and a relatively efficient government administration. Few other former colonies were left with such a favourable heritage by their colonial masters.

BRITISH COLONIALISM

The British, through its East India Company, expanded its influence over the Indian subcontinent from the 17th century, eventually assuming sovereignty over India in 1858 when the East India Company was abolished. To the east, the British annexed Burma in 1886 after a series of Anglo-Burmese wars, and it became a separate British colony (distinct from India) in 1935. Further east, between 1874 and 1914, the British slowly gained control of the states on the Malayan peninsular, first as protectorates, and later as colonies. During the period 1841–1946, North Borneo and Sarawak also became British colonies, whilst Brunei became a British protectorate. Thus, by the end of the Second World War, much of South and Southeast Asia had been colonised by the British.

In East Asia, the British (like other Western powers) tried to exert their influence over China, intending to open the country up for trade. This was strongly resisted by the weak Qing government, and after a number of wars (often provoked by the Western powers), the most important of which were the two Opium Wars (1839–42, and 1856–58), the island of Hong Kong was ceded in perpetuity to the British under the Treaty of Nanking (1842), while part of Kowloon (opposite Hong Kong) was given to the British under the Tientsin treaties (1858–60) (Hahn 1963: 1–25). After China's defeat at the hands of the Japanese during the Sino-Japanese War (1894–95), Western powers demanded additional concessions from a weakened China. This resulted in the British acquiring the New Territories (behind Kowloon) under a 100-year lease in 1898.

The British acquired their colonies primarily for the purpose of expanding British trade. They were interested in producing cash crops and extracting minerals for export (rather than in growing food for the home country), and in selling their manufactured goods (especially textiles) in their colonial markets. To this end, the small islands of Singapore and Hong Kong (both with deep, natural harbours and strategic locations) were developed into entrepots. Singapore was at the centre of Southeast Asia and on world sea routes between Europe and the Far East. Hong Kong was the gateway to China.

The importance of infrastructure (especially transport and communications) as well as literacy, for international trade was keenly appreciated by the British. To this end, they invested heavily in roads, railways, and harbours, and educated the local populations in their colonies in the language of international trade, science and technology, English.

In India, the British built roads and railways which formed a modern transport system, the basic features of which remain intact to this day. The first overland telegraph line between London and Calcutta was completed in 1865. Primary and secondary education was made available, and as a result, increasing numbers of Indians began to read and speak English, albeit with an accent which reflected the influence of Welsh missionaries. As early as 1835, English had already replaced Persian as India's official language. Whilst the British were keen to provide primary education to the masses (in order to service the lower rungs of government administration), secondary and tertiary education was restricted to the elite. In 1857, the first three universities were opened in Calcutta, Bombay and Madras. The British system of justice, based on the rule of law, was also established, and the Indian Civil Service was based on the Whitehall model.

As the British wanted to sell their textiles to the large Indian market, Indian tariffs were kept low in order to facilitate imports from Britain. One consequence of this was that the Indian textile industry was decimated as it was unable to compete with cheap imports from Britain. On the other hand, Indian raw cotton could be imported into Britain at negligible tariffs. This resulted in the Indian economy being developed along classic colonial lines, specialising in raw material exports and almost wholly dependent on manufactured imports from the home country.

A similar pattern of British investment occurred in its colonies in Southeast Asia. In Malaya, for example, the British built a modern transport system stretching from the north of the Malayan peninsula to the south. This north-south transport system was concentrated in the western half of the peninsula, since this was where most of the British-owned rubber estates and tin mines were located. The British did not develop east-west transport networks, since they had little commercial interests in the eastern part of the Malayan peninsula.

The north-south transport system ended in Singapore, which served as the main port through which raw material exports were shipped, and manufactured goods were imported. With this in mind, the British developed extensive port and storage facilites in Singapore, ship-handling and bunkering facilities to service the many ships which passed through Singapore, as well as banking and insurance industries to provide financial services to importers and exporters. As in India, the British system of justice and public administration was established in Malaya to provide the legal and administrative framework for commerce.

As a local labour force literate in English was required to operate the lower levels of commercial and government administration, the British invested in education, enabling the local population to acquire basic reading and writing skills in English. While primary education was made available, secondary and tertiary education was limited, as too much education for locals was thought to be politically undesirable. The precursors of the University of Malaya (established in 1949, and located in Singapore) appeared in the form of the establishment of the King Edward VII Medical College in 1905, and Raffles College in 1920. The latter was set up primarily to train teachers. The curriculum in higher education was strictly controlled by the colonial government. For many years, professors at Raffles College had no influence over the curricula and content of the subjects they taught.

DUTCH COLONIALISM

In 1602, the Dutch East India Company was formed. It undertook commercial ventures in South Asia for over a hundred years, but was eventually forced out by the British by the middle of the 18th century. The Dutch then turned their attention to Southeast Asia where they already had colonial interests. In 1619, the Dutch East India Company occupied a town in West Java and renamed it Batavia (now known as Jakarta). From then on, it slowly acquired more and more territory, establishing large plantations for the production of cash crops such as coffee and pepper. In 1798, the Dutch East India Company was dissolved after years of incurring financial losses, and the Dutch East Indies passed into the control of the Dutch government.

The Dutch were mainly interested in the East Indies for the raw material and spices that they could obtain there. They undertook relatively little infrastructural investment in the country (a notable exception being the Great Post Road which transversed the length of the island of Java), and did little to educate the local population (in 1947, on the eve of independence, some 63% of the population were illiterate (Booth 1998: 274)). Most of the trade which they carried out was undertaken by the Dutch themselves, or Chinese merchants. Indonesians were relegated mainly to the task of growing the crops (sometimes through coercive methods) that were to be exported.

Although per capita incomes in Indonesia did grow during the colonial period, it was slow and erratic, averaging 0.2% per annum during 1820–1900, and 0.3% per annum during 1900–50 (Booth 1998: 6). The integration of Indonesia into the world economy as a primary product exporter, resulted in large fluctuations in exports and incomes, and a secular decline in terms of trade (Booth 1998: 46–47). The living standards of a small minority of Indonesians improved under Dutch colonialism. For the vast majority, what data is available suggests that the opposite occurred (Booth 1998: 113–116).

FRENCH COLONIALISM

The French arrived in India in 1664, and ten years later, purchased the port of Pondicherry which they made into their headquarters. However, they never obtained a strong foothold in India, either in terms of trade or territory. What little they did control was handed over to the British at the end of the Napoleonic Wars.

The French were more successful in Southeast Asia where their influence grew in Vietnam, Laos and Cambodia. In 1802, the French helped Nguyen Anh regain the throne at Hue and were rewarded with territorial acquisitions. Similarly, in 1850, the French stood between rival factions in Cambodia, and extended their influence in that country. These were the beginnings of a long period of French influence in Indochina.

From the middle of the 19th century, the French continued to consolidate their presence in Indochina. As a result of a series of military successes over internal opposition, they were ceded more and more territory. In 1863, Cambodia came under French protection as a result of a request by its emperor, Norodom. By 1884, the French had secured almost complete control of Cambodia and Laos, and had annexed large parts of North Vietnam. In 1887, a unified French colonial administration was established in Indochina, marking the culmination of French colonisation in Southeast Asia.

The French monopolised economic activity in Indochina, controlling most of its finance and trade. In 1906, they introduced French education (along with Chinese, and romanised local languages), and also established tertiary education. But apart from this, they did little to develop their Southeast Asian colonies, and concentrated on the export of primary products from these territories.

SPANISH AND PORTUGUESE COLONIALISM

Portuguese penetration of Asia began in 1498, when Vasco da Gama reached the southwestern coast of India. In 1510, Alfonso de Albuquerque took the port of Goa, and made it into the centre of Portuguese activity in Asia. A year later, Albuquerque captured Malacca, on the southwest cost of the Malayan peninsula, destroying it in the process, but rebuilt it into the first city in Asia designed along European lines. From Malacca, the Portuguese sailed further east into China and Japan. The Portuguese did not hold large territories in Asia. In 1641, they lost Malacca to the Dutch, but held on to their remaining possessions of Goa, and the eastern half of the island of Timor.

About the same time that the Portuguese were venturing into Asia by sailing east around the Cape of Good Hope, the Spanish followed suit by sailing west through the Straits of Magellan. In 1519, Ferdinand Magellan reached the Philippines and landed on the island of Cebu. By 1571, the Spanish had established themselves at Manila, and over the next five years, most of the Philippines fell under their control (except the Muslim islands in the south). This was the start of a four-hundred-year period, during which the Hispanisation of the Philippines was accomplished.

Like the Portuguese, the Spanish were only interested in trade and did little to develop their Asian colonies. They brought their Catholic religion and their language, but little else to the people over whom they ruled. They imposed a feudal system of agriculture, transplanted from their home countries, and established large estates (owned by the Church as well as by favoured private individuals) many of which have survived to this day.

CONCLUSION

Economic development

Many countries in Southeast and East Asia benefited from their colonial period. South Korea and Taiwan benefited from Japanese investments in infrastructure, education, industrial development, and public administration. Similarly, Malaysia and Singapore benefited from British investments in these areas. India and Burma, which also inherited considerable infrastructural investments from the British, did not build on these in the post-independence period (certainly not to the extent to which Malaysia and Singapore did), and allowed their valuable assets to deteriorate. The Dutch, the Spanish, the Portuguese and the French did relatively little to develop their colonies in Southeast and East Asia. At the end of their respective colonial periods, Indonesia, the Philippines, and the Indo-Chinese states had progressed little from the underdeveloped state in which they were found by their colonial masters. This can be seen by a comparison of a number of selected development indicators of Southeast and East Asian countries in 1960 (comparable data for earlier years are not available). These are shown in Table 2.1.

TABLE 2.1: SOUTHEAST AND EAST ASIAN DEVELOPMENT, 1960

Country	Lit	LExp	InMort	Pop/Doc	Agr/LF	Ind/GDP	Pri/Exp	Energy
Bangladesh	26	47	139	9260	87	8	44	43
India	36	51	NA	5800	74	20	55	108
Pakistan	21	52	NA	11000	61	16	73	61
Sri Lanka	78	69	63	4500	56	22	99	107
Burma	67	53	NA	9900	68	12	99	55
Malaysia	60	67	31	6940	63	18	94	242
Singapore	75	70	31	2400	8	18	74	372
Indonesia	62	47	125	41000	75	14	100	129
Philippines	87	60	98	2760	61	28	96	147
Hong Kong	90	72	42	2990	8	34	20	468
South Korea	93	63	62	3000	66	19	86	258
Taiwan	77	64	NA	2243	50	27	68	420

Key: Lit=Adult literacy rate (%), LExp=Life expectancy (years), InMort=Infant
mortality (per 1000), Pop/Doc=Population per doctor, Agr/LF=Labour
force in agriculture (%), Ind/GDP=Industry share in GDP (%), Pri/
Exp=Primary product share in total exports (%), Energy=Energy
consumption per capita (kg oil equivalent)
Source: World Bank, *World Development Report* (various issues)

The first column of Table 2.1 shows that literacy rates (an
indicator of educational attainment) in South Asia were not very high
in 1960. Apart from Sri Lanka (and the southern Indian state of Kerala
which is not shown in the table), the other countries on the Indian
subcontinent had adult literacy rates ranging from 21% to 36%. In
Southeast Asia, high literacy rates were evident in Singapore and the
Philippines in 1960, but the other countries in the region exhibited
only moderate literacy rates. In East Asia, literacy rates in Hong Kong,
South Korea and Taiwan were already close to those of developed
countries in 1960. The high literacy rates of Singapore, Hong Kong,
South Korea and Taiwan are a reflection of the investment in primary
education they received during their colonial periods. While it was
relatively easy for the colonial governments to invest in education in
these relatively small countries, the low-to-moderate literacy rates in
other parts of South and Southeast Asia are an indication of the relative

effort and expense that colonial governments exerted in educating the people over whom they ruled.

Columns 2 to 4 are indicators of basic health care. With the exception of Sri Lanka, the other countries in South Asia have indices which show inadequate provision of basic health services (relatively low life expectancy, high infant mortality, and large numbers of people per doctor). This is an indication of poor investments in basic health infrastructure. Southeast Asian countries did not fare much better, apart from Malaysia and Singapore, whose relatively good scores in each of these indicators are similar to those of East Asian countries.

Columns 5 to 7 are indicators of economic structure. Column 5 shows that, with the exception of Singapore and Hong Kong, all the other countries in the table were agricultural economies in 1960. However, whereas agriculture in the countries in South Asia was predominantly subsistence agriculture, in many Southeast Asian countries, it was plantation agriculture producing food and primary products for export. This is reflected in the large percentage of primary products in total exports for most countries in the table, with Bangladesh and India being glaring exceptions. Column 6 shows that, with the exception of Hong Kong, the Philippines and Taiwan, industrial development was relatively slight in most of the countries in the region. This was a typical legacy of colonial economic development. The colonies were made to specialise in primary product exports, many of which were used in the metropolitan centres to make manufactured goods which were then exported to the colonies. Industrial development in the colonies was limited to products which had "natural protection" (such as building materials, bottles, etc., which were expensive to transport). This ensured that industrial development in the colonies would not compete with manufactured imports from the metropolitan centres. This gave rise to a "lop-sided" economic structure in many colonial economies, which remained primarily agricultural, and concentrated on primary product exports. While this brought prosperity to some colonial economies (such as Malaya), it had devastating effects in others (such as the Philippines) (Tiglao 1999: 63–65).

The last column of Table 2.1 is an indicator of infrastructural investment. High energy consumption is a reflection of the availability of electricity generating capacity. The high levels of per capita energy consumption in Singapore, Hong Kong, South Korea and Taiwan indicate, not only the availability of electricity generating capacity, but also a higher degree of industrial and commercial development. This is in sharp contrast to the very low per capita energy consumption levels in some South Asian countries. Other countries in the region (such as Sri Lanka, Malaysia, Indonesia and the Philippines) have higher per capita energy consumption levels, but even these are nowhere near the levels observed for Singapore and the East Asian countries.

In terms of economic development, the colonial heritage differs considerably between Asian countries. While the city states of Singapore and Hong Kong, and the other East Asian countries (South Korea and Taiwan) benefited from their colonial heritage in terms of infrastructural investment, educational attainment and commercial development, the same cannot be said of other South and Southeast Asian countries. One important factor which explains this is the reason for colonisation. Where colonies were acquired for the expansion of trade (as in Singapore and Hong Kong), or for the production of food (as in South Korea and Taiwan), the colonial powers often made large investment in infrastructure, education and agriculture. This was less likely to be the case where colonies were acquired primarily to extract raw materials, or to produce cash crops for exports. Thus, while living standards of the local people in some countries improved after decades of colonial domination, they declined in others.

Politics and government

Countries that were colonised by the British inherited the Westminster system of Prime Ministerial government. However, within a relatively short space of time, most of these had degenerated into military dictatorships, or one-party governments, with or without a veneer of democratic institutions (such as genuinely free elections, or an independent judiciary). One reason for this change was the perceived incompetence of politicians to manage the economy. This often prompted the military to seize power in order to the "save" the nation from economic collapse. Another reason was the lack of ability and talent of opposition leaders who were no match for some of the skilled and charismatic leaders that emerged after independence. Of the former British colonies in South and Southeast Asia, India remains the world's largest, working democracy.

In the Philippines, the influence of brief American colonial government left it with an American Presidential system of government (complete with all its warts). Apart from the 1972–86 period of martial law under President Marcos, the Philippines has remained one of the most democratic countries in Southeast Asia.

In Indonesia, a Presidential system of government was adopted at independence, but this soon changed to an authoritarian system of government under President Sukarno's "Guided Democracy", and later under President Suharto's "New Order". In 1998, Indonesia experienced a new age of democratic government following its first free elections since 1955, but the form which this might eventually take, and its consequences for the political development of the country are, as yet, unclear.

In the Indo-Chinese states, Communist governments were established, often after long armed struggles against colonial powers. Although the centrally-planned economies which they implemented have largely disappeared, the totalitarian form of centralised government that is typical of Communist states, still prevails.

The countries of Asia which had to fight for their independence have important differences with those that were granted their independence through a peaceful transfer of power. Those that had to fight for their independence often maintained a hostile attitude towards Western countries (and, of course, especially towards their former colonial masters). Trade, commerce, investment, cultural exchange, and other forms of interaction with the former colonial powers were often curtailed, or at least not encouraged. Education systems were changed in favour of a local, national language (in this respect, it is curious that the Indonesians have not expunged many

Dutch words from Bahasa Indonesia). Countries that were granted their independence through a peaceful transfer of power have often maintained cordial economic and cultural links with their former colonial masters. Some have even retained the language of their former colonial powers, or have at least given it equal status with that of their national language.

The colonial heritage has been an important factor in the subsequent development of Asian countries. This is a theme to which we will return in the following chapters.

CHAPTER 3

Changes in Economic Structure

INTRODUCTION

One of the most important changes in the development of Asian countries since the Second World War has been in their economic structure. Since gaining independence, many Asian countries diversified their economies away from agriculture towards industry.

In the 1950s and 1960s, industrialisation was accomplished by implementing import-substitution policies, but by the mid-1980s, most Asian countries had shifted to export-oriented industrialisation. This shift was often accompanied by a movement away from centralised, state-dominated economies towards decentralised, market-oriented economies. Even Communist regimes abandoned central-planning and embraced market-oriented economic reforms.

Within agriculture, the most important development in Asian countries was the introduction of high-yielding varieties of wheat and rice known as the "Green Revolution".

By the 1990s, some Asian countries had developed so successfully that they began to display a "post-industrial" economic structure in which services were the most important sector of their economies.

FROM AGRICULTURE TO INDUSTRY

As explained in the previous chapter, colonialisation left many Asian countries with "lop-sided" economic structures. Most of the economic activities in these countries were concentrated on primary product exports. Industry was relatively underdeveloped, and most manufactured goods had to be imported (often) from the metropolitan centres.

This heavy reliance on primary product exports had some unfortunate consequences. The prices of primary products (such as rubber or coffee) had the tendency to fluctuate markedly from season to season, affected by changes in demand and supply conditions. This "export instability" was thought to be undesirable and harmful to primary product exporters. It was also thought that the prices of primary product exports tended not to rise as fast as the prices of manufactured imports, causing a secular decline in terms of trade. Over the long term, this would put primary product exporters at an increasing disadvantage, as they would have to export more and more commodities in order to purchase the same amount of manufactured imports. Too great a reliance on agriculture was also thought to be undesirable because agricultural activities could not create new jobs fast enough to absorb the growing labour forces of many Asian countries. For these reasons, many countries embarked on a programme of industrialisation soon after gaining independence. The shift away from agriculture towards industry would not only help to diversify the economic structure, but would also assist in creating new jobs for a growing labour force. This would be accomplished by expanding the industrial sector through new investments that would, at the same time, reduce the relative size of the agricultural sector (Oshima 1986: 783–809). The extent to which many Asian countries accomplished this economic transformation successfully can be seen in Figure 3.1.

Figure 3.1 shows that in 1970, India (which was typical of countries in South Asia), China, Vietnam (which was typical of countries in Indochina), and Indonesia (which was typical of countries in Southeast Asia, except Singapore) were still predominantly agricultural economies. Between two-thirds and four-fifths of their labour forces were engaged in agriculture. East Asian economies (represented by South Korea in Figure 3.1, and excepting Hong Kong) were less dependent on agriculture as they were already more industrialised, but about half their labour forces were still engaged in agriculture in 1970.

FIGURE 3.1: THE DECLINE OF AGRICULTURE

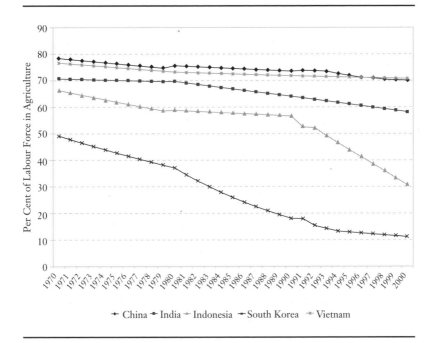

Source: World Bank, *World Development Indicators 2002*

Over the next 30 years, East Asian economies (such as South Korea) industrialised rapidly, so that by 2000, only about 10% of their labour forces were engaged in agriculture. Most of the labour that left the agriculture sector were employed in the industrial sector. The city states of Singapore and Hong Kong are exceptions, since they had very small agricultural sectors to begin with.

The shift away from agriculture to industry was less pronounced in Southeast Asia. In the case of Indonesia, the percentage of the labour force engaged in agriculture fell steadily in the 1970s and 1980s, but this decline did not begin to accelerate until the early 1990s. One reason for this is that, unlike East Asian economies, Southeast Asian economies were rich in natural resources and primary product exports. There was less need to industrialise in order to earn foreign exchange to finance imports.

Figure 3.1 shows that the shift from agriculture to industry was least pronounced in South Asia (represented by India) and the Communist states (represented by China and Vietnam). In 2000, most of their labour forces were still engaged in agricultural activities, in spite of rapid industrialisation (in China specially after 1978, and in Vietnam especially after 1983). The same is true of Myanmar, which was closed to the rest of the world by its military rulers since the 1950s, and has languished as a poor, agricultural economy ever since. In 1990, 73% of its labour force was engaged in agriculture. By early 2000, however, rapid industrialization in China had resulted in large numbers of people leaving the countryside for the cities. Even though just under 70% of China's population was located in rural areas, its large population size meant that there were some 120 million rural migrants living in towns and cities, and this figure is expected to rise in the future (Hsieh 2002: A3).

Over the same period of time (1970–2000), industry accounted for a growing share of the total output of all Asian countries (except Myanmar). By 2000, the share of industry in Gross Domestic Product (GDP) was 43% in South Korea, 47% in Indonesia, 37% in Vietnam, 27% in India, and 35% in China. By this time, many Asian countries had large industrial sectors, and had become important world producers of many manufactured products. Myanmar, however, has remained an agricultural economy. In 2000, industry accounted for only 7% of its GDP. Closed to the outside world, and shunned by the international community as a pariah state, it has remained one of the poorest, agricultural economies in the world.

FROM IMPORT-SUBSTITUTION TO EXPORT-ORIENTED INDUSTRIALISATION

Import-substitution

In the 1950s and 1960s, industrialisation in many Asian countries was accomplished by implementing a strategy of import-substitution. This was done by preventing the imports of certain manufactured products, and producing these products domestically. In this manner, domestically produced goods were substituted for imported products. Instead of importing, say, motor cars from Britain, a country like Malaysia would stop the import of cars, and manufacture cars locally for the domestic market. This would stimulate industrial development, create jobs and save foreign exchange.

Imports would be prevented from entering a country by the imposition of various trade barriers, the most important of which were taxes on imports called tariffs. This would raise the price of imports in the domestic market. An appropriately high tariff could be imposed so that the prices of the imported products would be so high as to eliminate imports completely. Alternatively, a quota might be imposed on the imports of a particular product. This would restrict the quantity of the products that could be imported. An appropriately small quota would eliminate imports of a product for all intents and purposes. Import barriers such as tariffs and quotas would normally be used against products which were previously imported in large volumes, since this indicated that there was a large domestic market for these products.

Data on tariffs are difficult to obtain especially for the 1950s or 1960s. As an illustration of the differences in tariffs imposed by Asian countries, data pertaining to import duties for 1980 (when some were still implementing import-substitution) are shown in Figure 3.2.

Figure 3.2 shows that, even in 1980, several Asian countries had relatively high rates of tariff protection which were reflected in high ratios of import duties to total import values. India and Pakistan fall into this category. Import-substitution in these countries is reflected by their relatively low import intensities (as measured by the ratio of imports to GDP). Taiwan is an exception since most of its tariffs are on the import of agricultural products (rather than manufactured goods). It has a relatively high ratio of import duties to total imports as well as a high ratio of imports to GDP (the latter is a consequence of the high import dependence of its export-oriented manufacturing industries). The city-states of Singapore and Hong Kong have not been shown in Figure 3.2 since their very small ratios of import duties to total imports (0.9% for Singapore), and their very high ratios of imports to GDP (204% for Singapore) would distort the appearance of the scatter diagram considerably.

FIGURE 3.2: IMPORT DUTIES AND IMPORT INTENSITY, 1980

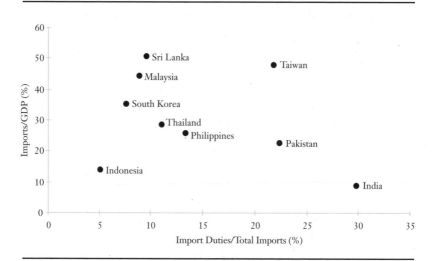

Sources: World Bank, *World Development Indicators 1999* (New York: Oxford University Press); Council for Economic Planning and Development, *Taiwan Statistical Data Book 1998* (Taipei: Council for Economic Development and Planning)

At the other end of the spectrum are Asian countries with relatively low ratios of import duties to total imports. These have moved away from import-substitution and gone into export-oriented industrialisation. The Philippines, South Korea, Thailand and Malaysia are in this category. Their low ratios of import duties to total imports are associated with relatively high ratios of imports to GDP. Indonesia is an exception as it has a relatively low ratio of import duties to total imports, as well as a relatively low ratio of imports to GDP. One possible reason for this is that tariffs are not the main barriers to imports in Indonesia. Various non-tariff barriers may be more important in keeping imports out. In spite of the presence of a few "outliers", Figure 3.2 does confirm a broad negative relationship between tariff barriers and import intensity.

The initial impact of import-substitution in many Asian countries was impressive. Since the domestic market had been protected by tariffs, locally established firms had a virtual monopoly over consumers, and industrial production grew rapidly in the first few years (the "exhilaration phase") after import-substitution was implemented. Double-digit rates of growth of manufacturing output were common. However, within a decade or so, the small domestic market became saturated, as most people had already bought the domestically made product. Further growth in demand could only come through replacement purchases (which were relatively few in the case of durable consumption goods such as air conditioners), or population and income growth. The consequence of this was that the growth of the manufacturing sector slowed down, and economic growth began to stagnate. Thus, import-substitution turned out to be a "self-terminating" industrialisation strategy. This is illustrated in Figure 3.3, which shows the growth rate of manufacturing output in the Philippines during 1951–65, when it implemented import-substitution.

FIGURE 3.3: GROWTH OF MANUFACTURING OUTPUT IN THE PHILIPPINES, 1951–65

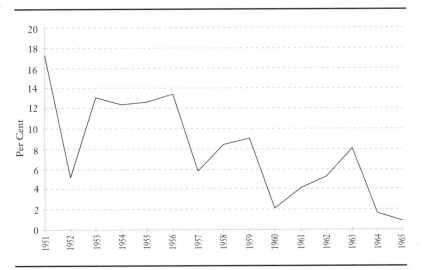

Source: Paauw and Fei (1973), p. 268

In the early 1950s, the growth of manufacturing output in the Philippines was (with rare exceptions) in double digits. By the late 1950s, manufacturing output growth began to slow down, as the domestic market approached saturation. By 1965, manufacturing output growth had stagnated at less than 1% per annum. The high growth rates of output of the manufacturing sector that were experienced in the early phases of import-substitution could not be sustained. Many Asian countries which implemented import-substitution experienced this pattern of industrial growth.

Once a country has reached the end of what is known as the "first stage" of import-substitution (which concentrates on the manufacture of final consumer goods), there are two alternatives which might be pursued. One is to embark on "second stage" import-substitution, in which the domestic manufacture of capital and intermediate goods is attempted through tariff protection. Instead of making, say, cars, a country might make steel which is used in the manufacture of cars. Very few countries have done this successfully, since second stage import-substitution is much more difficult than first stage import-substitution. The capital requirements (in terms of the scale of investment involved) are much higher, the skill requirements (in terms of engineers, scientists, management personnel, etc.) are also much higher, and the minimum output required to achieve minimum average costs is much larger than can be absorbed in the domestic market. For these reasons, it is usually much more difficult for a country to implement second stage import-substitution than it is to implement first stage import-substitution.

The other alternative is to embark on export-oriented industrialisation. Since the domestic market is too small to absorb its manufactured output, selling to the world market might be a way of avoiding this constraint. Unfortunately, it is extremely difficult to convert import-substituting manufacturing firms into export-oriented firms. The main reason for this is that import-substituting firms tend to be relatively high-cost and inefficient, by world standards. Being protected from international competition by tariffs, import-substituting firms are able to operate at inefficient scales of output, and survive in the domestic market, even though their average costs of production are very much higher than world prices. This would make their products uncompetitive in world markets.

In order to convert import-substituting firms into export-oriented firms, tariffs would have to be reduced, high-cost, inefficient firms would have to be closed down, and only those that are able to compete effectively in world markets would be allowed to remain. This would, necessarily, create considerable unemployment in the short to medium term, and is often politically and socially unacceptable, especially in countries in which governments have to be periodically re-elected. In less developed countries, where government ministers and officials (and/or their relative and friends) own import-substituting firms, the pressure to maintain, or increase (rather than reduce), tariffs would be difficult to resist. Thus, many countries in Asia that implemented import-substitution in the 1950s became stuck at the end of the first stage of import-substitution, unable to move into second stage import-substitution, or to convert their industries into export-oriented ones.

Export-oriented industrialisation

Export-oriented industrialisation, by its very nature, tends to avoid many of the disadvantages of import-substitution. By focusing on the world market, export-oriented industrialisation avoids the problem of domestic market saturation. By competing with the best in the world, export-oriented firms are forced to become internationally competitive in order to survive in the international marketplace. Unlike import-substitution, export-oriented industrialisation does not provide protection for high-cost, inefficient firms. Nevertheless, as pointed out in the previous section, it is extremely difficult to implement export-oriented industrialisation, especially when a country has previously implemented import-substitution.

THE NEWLY INDUSTRIALISING
COUNTRIES OF ASIA

In Asia, three countries achieved the transformation from import-substitution to export-oriented industrialisation in the 1960s. Together with Hong Kong SAR (which never implemented import-substitution), Singapore, South Korea and Taiwan (which are collectively known as Newly Industrialising Countries (NICs) of Asia) were the first of the less developed countries in Asia to achieve this transition successfully.

South Korea and Taiwan had implemented import-substitution after the Second World War when large amounts of Amercian aid were used to import capital and intermediate goods for their domestic manufacturing industries. By the early 1960s, both countries could see the beginnings of domestic market saturation. In Taiwan, for example, the growth rate of manufacturing output was 32.5% per annum in 1952, but by 1960, had more than halved to 14.2% per annum. In addition, by the late 1950s, the Americans had announced that they were terminating their foreign aid programme to both South Korea and Taiwan in the early 1960s. This meant that American funds would no longer be available to support their import-substituting industries. Both countries then began to implement policies designed to convert their industries from import-substituting to export-oriented ones.

There were a number of important reasons that explain why South Korea and Taiwan were able to implement the painful measures that were required to implement export-oriented industrialisation. In 1962, General Park Chung Hee seized power in a *coup d'etat*, and proclaimed martial law. Taiwan had been a military dictatorship ever since General Chiang Kai Shek fled to the island with his followers in 1949, after having lost the civil war to the Communists in China. Following initial resistance to the mainlanders from the Taiwanese, General Chiang also declared martial law in Taiwan. Under strong, authoritarian governments, the painful measures that were required to convert their manufacturing sectors to export-oriented ones could be implemented in South Korea and Taiwan without much opposition.

In addition, world trade was growing rapidly in the 1960s, and with the help of the Cold War politics (which persuaded the Americans to give South Korea and Taiwan preferential access to the US market), the unemployment created by the dismantling of import-substitution were quickly re-absorbed in export-oriented industries. Thus, the transition from import-substitution to export-oriented industrialisation was less painful for South Korea and Taiwan than it might otherwise have been. This is reflected in the speed with which both countries reduced tariffs and other barriers to imports. This is illustrated in Figure 3.4, which shows the percentage of South Korean import items not subject to quotas.

FIGURE 3.4: SOUTH KOREAN NON-QUOTA IMPORT ITEMS

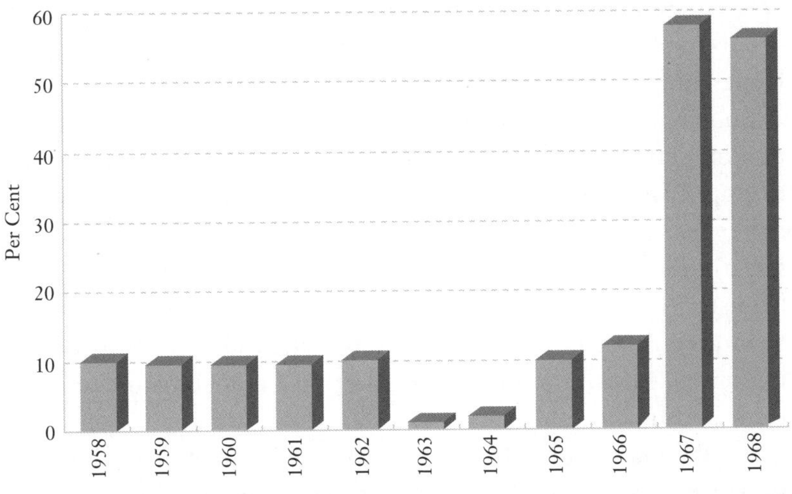

Source: World Bank, *World Development Report 1987*, p. 100

In the late 1950s, only about 10% of South Korea's imports were not subject to quota restrictions. Between 1965 and 1968, this increased to nearly 60%, and by 1984, had reached 85% (not shown in Figure 3.4). South Korea's nominal tariffs, which averaged 68% in 1959, fell to 35% in 1961 and after a period of increases during the 1970s (during which South Korea implemented a heavy industry development programme), decreased to 30% in 1984 (World Bank 1987: 100).

Singapore, like Hong Kong SAR, had been established as a free port when the British colonised it in 1819. As such, tariff protection had always been negligible, considering Singapore's very small domestic market. Nevertheless, during the late 1950s and early 1960s, Singapore did implement an import-substitution industrialisation strategy as it anticipated being merged with Malaya (as it was known then), and could look forward to a much larger combined market. Singapore's membership of the larger Federation of Malaysia (which also included the eastern states of Sabah and Sarawak) was short-lived. Owing to irreconcilable political differences, Singapore was forced to leave the Federation of Malaysia in 1965, and contemplate its political as well as economic survival as an independent island state, cut off from its economic hinterland. This forced the Singapore government to launch into an export-oriented industrialisation strategy. As tariffs in Singapore were never very high (in the early 1960s, the average nominal tariff rate was less than 1%), its transition to an export-oriented industrial economy was not as difficult as it might otherwise have been. Furthermore, a strong and efficient government under the charismatic leadership of the (then) Prime Minister, Lee Kuan Yew, made it possible to implement whatever economic reforms were necessary to turn the city state into an important part of the international grid of global manufacturing, trade and finance.

Although Hong Kong SAR never implemented import-substitution, its shift from an entrepot through which most of China's trade with other countries passed, began in 1966 when Chairman Mao launched the Cultural Revolution on the mainland. One important impact of this was to reduce, significantly, Hong Kong SAR's role as an entrepot as China retreated into virtual autarchy under the influence of the Gang of Four and the Red Guards. Another consequence of the political turmoil in China, was the flood of refugees which swept into Hong Kong SAR (providing it with large amounts of cheap labour). The reduction in entrepot trade forced Hong Kong SAR to embark on export-oriented industrialisation, and the influx of refugees from China gave it the comparative advantage it needed in labour-intensive manufactured exports.

THE ASEAN COUNTRIES

In Southeast Asia, the countries which were members of the Association of Southeast Asian Nations (ASEAN), which included, amongst others, Thailand, Malaysia, Indonesia, developed during the 1950–85 period, on the back of primary product exports (such as rubber, tin, copra, palm oil, etc.) and (in the case of Indonesia and Malaysia) petroleum exports. These enabled them to earn large amounts of foreign exchange to finance their import-substituting industries.

By the early 1980s, the world price of petroleum started to decline from its peak of US$38 per barrel in 1981. The export prices of all other primary commodities also declined. This put pressure on many ASEAN countries to seek other sources of foreign exchange earnings to finance their development.

In 1985, the Plaza Agreement was signed by the G5 countries (which included the USA, UK, Germany, Italy and Japan). In a bid to reduce USA's trade deficit with Japan, the central banks of these countries agreed to force an upvaluation of the Japanese yen relative to the US dollar. By 1988, the yen had appreciated by 100% and was still rising in value, causing tremendous dislocation in Japanese industry, and Japanese exports. The Japanese reacted by moving their relatively inefficient industries offshore where wages and exchange rates were more favourable, and productivity was relatively high. Thailand, Malaysia and Indonesia were ideal locations for this purpose.

About the same time, all the Asian NICs were facing labour shortages and rising wages as a result of declining fertility and rapid economic growth. This prompted them to move their more labour-intensive industries (such as clothing and footwear) to other countries where wages were lower, and productivity levels were favourable. Again, Thailand, Malaysia and Indonesia were favourite destinations to which the Asian NICs moved their relatively inefficient industries.

Thus, between 1985 and 1990, Thailand, Malaysia and Indonesia experienced large inflows of foreign investment from Japan and the Asian NICs. This propelled these countries into export-oriented industrialisation.

The Philippines did not benefit from these developments as much as Thailand, Malaysia or Indonesia. Political instability after the Aquino government came to power in 1986, a virtual breakdown of law and order (with frequent kidnapping of business executives), poor infrastructure, as well as a series of natural disasters (volcanic eruptions, typhoons, etc.) made the Philippines an unfavourable destination for foreign investment.

CHINA, INDOCHINA AND SOUTH ASIA

The changes in the international economy that took place in the mid-1980s also spilled over into China, Indochina (especially Vietnam) and South Asia. In the latter half of the 1980s, the Asian NICs (especially Hong Kong SAR and Taiwan) moved much of their labour-intensive industries into southern China, transforming the southern provinces of Guandong and Fujian into export-oriented manufacturing sites (East Asia Analytical Unit 1992). A similar development occurred in Vietnam after 1983 when the *doi moi* economic reforms opened the country up to foreign investment and trade. In South Asia, a change of government in 1991 ended decades of inward-looking economic policies in India, and started a process of economic reform towards greater export orientation, inward foreign investment and trade. Similar changes occurred in Bangladesh and Pakistan. However, South Asia's transition from import-substitution to export-oriented industrialisation has not been as rapid as in China or Vietnam. Weak governments, political instablity, and poor infrastructure have made progress in this direction slow.

From regulated to market-oriented economies

One important aspect of the transformation from import-substitution to export-oriented industrialisation in Asian countries has been the shift from centralised, regulated, state-dominated economies to decentralised, deregulated, market-oriented economies.

Under import-substitution, the government regulated much of the economic activity. Tariffs were imposed, quotas were set, import licences were granted, interest rates were kept low, wage levels were set, capital flows were regulated, and the foreign exchange rate was often maintained at a rate that was above what the market would have determined (this was done to make the import of capital and intermediate goods relatively cheap). Market forces were not allowed to determine relative prices which were distorted by government interventions. As explained above, these distortions resulted in a misallocation of scarce resources and widespread inefficiencies.

The epitome of a state-controlled, regulated economy was the centrally-planned economy that was found in many Communist states in Asia and Eastern Europe. Under central planning, the state set the prices of all major commodities (often, without any regard for relative scarcities), determined all outputs, allocated all resources (including labour) administratively, owned all property, and controlled foreign trade. Markets were not allowed to determine relative prices, wages, profits, or the composition of output. All economic activity had to conform to a central plan. Wage rates were set without any regard for differences in ability or productivity. Any profits earned by firms had to be surrendered to the state. There was therefore no incentive to do more than the minimum required. This led to a massive misallocation of resources, and large inefficiencies, both at the micro as well as the macro level (Nove 1983: 68–117).

The transition to export-oriented industrialisation required deregulation of the economy through market-oriented reforms. In order for a country to capitalise on its comparative advantage, markets need to be allowed to work efficiently in order to provide the correct price signals that would guide the allocation of scarce resources towards areas in which a country does have, or can develop, a high level of international competitiveness.

In the area of trade, this meant removing tariffs and quotas, floating the foreign exchange rate, and abolishing subsidies. In the labour market, wages had to be determined by the forces of demand and supply, rather than by governments or trade unions. In industry, firms had to be given the freedom to choose their inputs and outputs, and to determine their production techniques. In finance, interest rates had to be deregulated, and restrictions of capital flows removed. The implementation of these market-oriented reforms would open the economy to the forces of international competition, and make it a participant in the global economy. In the words of one proponent of this view, "As long as reasonably sensible policies are in place, if [a country] makes use of — that is, genuinely opens itself up to — the global economy, prosperity follows." "The effectiveness of region states is to depend on their ability to tap global solutions. It is to improve the quality of their peoples' lives by attracting and harnessing the talents and resources of the global economy, not by warding that economy off so that special interests can flourish." (Ohmae 1975: 23, 96).

With the possible exception of Hong Kong SAR, all the other Asian NICs were characterised by a combination of varying degrees of state intervention and the operation of relatively free markets. The view that they were completely free market economies in which the state played a minimalist role is a myth (Lim 1983: 752–64). The state orchestrated the exported-oriented industrialisation strategy, directed the provision of finance into favoured areas and firms, controlled the labour market to ensure that wages did not rise too quickly, and often participated directly in industrial or commercial activities. In areas (such as agriculture) where the country had no comparative advantage, tariffs and other barriers to imports remained high to protect domestic producers. So, although governments in the Asian NICs (Hong Kong SAR excepted) deregulated their trade sectors, they played an important role in economic affairs. This was most pronounced in South Korea and Taiwan, and least pronounced in Hong Kong SAR (with Singapore occupying an intermediate position). However, the role of the state was often exercised through (rather than in opposition to) the operation of markets. The state often used the price mechanism to achieve its goals. For example, when wages were kept down, or prevented from rising too rapidly, this worked through the labour market by encouraging firms to employ more labour. Thus, most of the Asian NICs could be characterised as economies which combined "technocratic economic rationalism with paternalistic authoritarianism" (Fukuyama 1992: 243).

In the ASEAN countries (and especially in Malaysia and Indonesia), authoritarian governments controlled all the levers of power, but intervened less pervasively in economic affairs than in the Asian NICs. Strong governments developed the strategies and planned the wars, but the private sector was left to execute the battles in ways in which they saw fit. While firms which were either owned by the government, or by private entreprenuers who were closely linked to the government, played an important role in these economies, they were only a part of a much larger, vibrant, private sector.

This was less evident in Thailand and the Philippines, where relatively weak governments played a much less important role in economic affairs.

Although export-oriented industralisation policies had been put in place in many ASEAN countries in the 1970s, these were not pursued with great vigour until the 1980s, when the prices of oil and other primary product exports began to fall, and the need to earn foreign exchange by other means became pressing. This prompted a series of market-oriented economic reforms in these countries in order to boost the activities of export-oriented manufacturing firms, many of which were being transferred from Japan and the Asian NICs in the second half of the 1980s.

In Indonesia, for example, the over-valued rupiah was devalued in 1983 and 1986 in order to make exports more competitive. Major reforms of the banking system were implemented in 1983 and 1988 in order to generate greater competition through an increase in the number of banks. In 1985, Indonesia's corrupt and inefficient customs services were put under the control of a Swiss company, SGS. A drawback system was implemented in order to enable exporters to import their inputs free of tariffs. Foreign investment rules were liberalised and eventually abolished. By the late 1980s, Indonesia had largely deregulated its economy, and was fast becoming a major exporter of labour-intensive manufactured goods (Hill and Suphalachalasai 1992: 310–29).

The most dramatic shifts from regulated to market-oriented economies occurred in the Communist states of Southeast and East Asia. In China, the death of Chairman Mao and the arrest of the Gang of Four, led to the end of the Cultural Revolution. By 1978, Deng Xiaoping was firmly in power, and instituted a series of market-oriented reforms which resulted in a gradual dismantling of the centrally-planned economic system. In agriculture, a "Production Responsibility System" was introduced. This allowed peasants to enter into contracts to supply the state with produce, and allowed them to sell any above-contract output to the state at higher prices or in free markets. This effectively restored the link between income and productivity which had been broken under central planning, and provided the material incentives to increase production. Similar market-oriented reforms were carried out in industry. Firms were given greater financial autonomy, allowing them to retain part of their profits, decide on the purchase of their inputs as well as the sales of their outputs, and pay bonuses for improved productivity. As in agriculture, this re-established the link between effort and income, and provided the material incentive that was sorely lacking under central planning. These market-oriented reforms were not as successful in industry as they were in agriculture. Within the industrial sector, the reforms were not as successful in state-owned firms as they were in collectively-owned, or privately-owned firms. In trade and investment, the monopoly of the powerful Ministry of Foreign Affairs and Trade (MOFERT) was broken and its functions decentralised. Foreign investment was allowed for the first time since the Communist revolution (Garnaut and Liu 1992: 6–48, 79–97). The impact of these market-oriented reforms was a large inflow of foreign investment into China, especially from Hong Kong SAR and Taiwan. This transformed the southern provinces of Guandong and Fujian into major world producers and labour-intensive manufacturing exporters in the 1980s and later spread into the interior provinces.

In the former Indo-Chinese states, the demise of Communism in Eastern Europe in the late 1980s cut off their main source of financial aid (mainly from the former Soviet Union) which underpinned their economies (mainly by financing imports). This made it necessary for these countries to look for other means of earning foreign exchange. At the same time, the gross inefficiencies of a centrally-planned economy had already caused serious concern in many of these countries. Agricultural output had been declining, agricultural collectivisation was being resented and resisted by the peasants, and state-run industries were hopelessly inefficient.

Although some economic reforms had been initiated in the late 1970s, the transition towards a market-oriented economic system was not accelerated until about the mid-1980s. In agriculture, all the former Indo-Chinese countries gradually moved away from collectivisation towards family-based production, giving peasants land-use rights which could be transferred, rented, inherited or mortgaged. Although in theory, the state owned all property, in practice, there was little difference (in the view of the peasants) between land-use rights and private ownership of land. In addition, peasants were often allowed to decide on what to produce, and to whom to sell their output. By the late 1980s, agriculture in Vietnam, Laos and Cambodia had been largely transformed from a collectivised system to a system based on household production operating in relatively free markets (St John 1997: 173–177).

In the industrial sector, economic reforms centred on granting firms greater financial autonomy in what outputs they produced, what inputs they used, what prices they charged, and to whom they sold. They were no longer required to meet mandatory targets prescribed by a central plan. In many cases, profits could be retained by the firm rather than surrendered to the state, and subsidies from the state were abolished. In Laos and Cambodia (and to a lesser extent, in Vietnam), the privatisation of state-owned enterprises was seen as a means to increasing efficiency and profitability (St John 1997: 77–181).

In trade, restrictive policies which had been implemented under
import-subsitution were relaxed, and laws were enacted to encourage
foreign investment (often in the form of joint ventures). The opening
up of the economies of Vietnam, Laos and Cambodia in the latter
part of the1980s also required reforms in banking and finance. The
banking systems of these countries were strengthened, and foreign
banks were allowed to operate in the domestic economy.

By the early 1990s, the Communist states of Southeast and East
Asia had, for all intents and purposes, abandoned central planning,
and moved toward market-oriented economic systems. As part of this
process, they became more closely integrated into the world economy
through trade and investment. However, the Communist parties in
these countries still retained their monopoly on political power.
Liberalisation was encouraged in economic affairs, but strongly
resisted in politics. The Tiananmen massacre in June 1989 is a constant
reminder of this.

The Green Revolution in agriculture

One important aspect of the development of Asian countries since
1950 has been the development of agriculture. In the 1950s and 1960s,
rapid population growth in many parts of Asia was viewed with alarm,
as it was widely feared that food production would not be able to
keep up with the increase in population. Social unrest and mass
starvation could be the likely consequences if either population growth
were not checked, or food production was not increased significantly.
The alternative of importing large amounts of food to feed growing
populations was not financially viable as a long-term solution to rapid
population growth.

With respect to food production (reducing population growth
will be discussed in a subsequent chapter), the problem in many
Asian countries lay in low productivity, and the difficulties of
increasing productivity in food production. Low productivity, in
many countries, was primarily due to a large number of subsistence
farmers and share-croppers often working very small plots (usually
less than half a hectare) of land (a legacy of an unequal distribution

of land). There was often no money, or incentive, to improve the land. In addition, decades of import-substituting industrialisation in many countries resulted in a neglect (and often, a penalisation) of agriculture. Widespread poverty in rural areas also had important political consequences. In the 1950s and 1960s, many Southeast Asian countries were fighting Communist insurgencies who drew their support primarily from the peasants. It was widely feared that, unless the living standards of the rural poor were improved significantly, the chances of winning the war against Communism were slim. The prospect of a "red" revolution sweeping through Asia caused considerable alarm.

The central problem lay in raising productivity in agriculture. One important way of doing this was to apply modern inputs, such as chemical fertilisers. However, traditional varieties of crops (such as wheat or rice) were not very responsive to increased chemical fertiliser input. Some increases in yield were possible, but these soon declined as more and more chemical fertilisers were applied.

In the early 1960s, an agricultural research facility was established at Los Banos in the Philippines, with the help of US money (mainly from the Ford and Rockerfeller Foundations). Its mission was to apply technological breakthroughs in developing High-Yielding Varieties (HYVs) of corn that had been achieved in the 1940s in Latin America, to rice and wheat production in Asia. If successful, these HYVs could result in a "green" revolution in Asia, which would effectively preempt a "red" revolution from taking place.

Characteristics of high-yielding varieties

The high-yielding varieties (which concentrated on rice in Southeast Asia) had a number of important characteristics, which themselves had significant social and economic implications.

First, the HYVs were highly responsive to chemical fertiliser input. In some varieties, yields continued to increase as more and more fertiliser was applied. This had important economic, as well as environmental, implications. Heavy fertiliser usage meant that this new technology was expensive to use, and could be environmentally

41

damaging since the production of chemical fertilisers is energy-intensive, and the extensive use of chemical fertilisers could pollute rivers and waterways.

Second, the heavy use of chemical fertilisers meant that water control was critical. Without the ability to apply the right amount of water, at the right time, farmers would not be able to reap the full benefits of the new technology. The implication of this was that certain countries, or regions within countries, would be more able to utilise HYVs, because they had good irrigation facilities. This could lead to a widening of regional income disparities.

Third, the HYVs were shorter and sturdier plants, which grew to approximately the same height, and ripened evenly, making them more amenable to mechanical harvesting. This had important consequences for the employment of labour.

Fourth, the HYVs had a shorter growing season, and were less photosensitive to the hours of daylight. This meant that multiple-cropping was possible. One important implication of this was that farmers would be encouraged to mechanise harvesting, and the preparation of land for the next crop. This would have important implications for labour absorption.

Fifth, HYVs were thought to be "neutral to scale". This meant that similar increases in yields could be obtained, irrespective of the farm size on which the HYVs were grown. In this respect, large farmers would not be able to benefit from the new technology disproportionately, compared with small farmers. If this were to be the case, the distribution of income was not likely to be adversely affected by the introduction of the new technology.

Sixth, the HYVs, being hybrid plants, did not have any natural protection (unlike traditional varieties) from fungi and pest attack. This required the application of chemicals to protect the plants from being devastated by such attacks. However, chemical usage for this purpose could aggravate the environmental damage caused by this new technology.

Seventh, the heavy application of chemical fertiliser increased not only crop yields, but the proliferation of weeds. Where chemicals were used to control weeds, the adverse environment consequences of this new technology could be further magnified. Where labour was used to control weeds, the employment effects of the new technology could be enhanced.

Thus, the HYVs had a number of characteristics which had important economic and social consequences. Some of these (such as the ability to produce more than one crop per year) were positive, while others (such as increased mechanisation or environment pollution) were negative. Some negative impacts of the HYVs were due, not to the new technology *per se*, but to the economic, social, and political environment in which it was applied. For example, in some countries, mechanisation was utilised much too rapidly after HYVs were introduced, not because of the new technology as such, but because governments offered cheap loans for the purchase of tractors. It is therefore important to bear in mind that the impacts of the new technology are often affected by the economic, social and political milieu into which it is introduced.

Impacts of the Green Revolution

There is little doubt that, in terms of food production, the Green Revolution was spectacularly successful. Large increases in yields were obtained once the new technology spread through many Asian countries after 1965, when they were first introduced on a large scale. In Indonesia, for example, rice yields in Java increased from 2.6 tons per hectare in 1970 to 5 tons per hectare in 1990. Over the same period of time, rice yields outside Java increased from 2 tons per hectare to 3.5 tons per hectare. By the mid-1980s, Indonesia was 99% self-sufficient in rice production, and in some years of good harvests, even exported rice (in sharp contrast to the 1950s and 1960s, when it was the world's largest rice importer). Living standards in rural Indonesia rose steadily as the incidence of poverty declined sharply (Economist 1979:48–50; Tjondronegoro et al. 1992: 71, 74). Similar improvements have been observed in other South and Southeast Asian countries or regions that have implemented HYVs (Blyn 1983: 705–25; Hazell and Ramaswamy 1991).

43

A large number of studies have been carried out on the question of labour absorption. The majority of these conclude that, on balance, the Green Revolution has been net labour-absorbing rather than labour-displacing. Although mechanisation has occurred, both in land preparation and harvesting, other pre-harvest and post-harvest activities as well as multiple-cropping, have resulted in a net increase in the demand for labour. This has been complemented by the large number of off-farm employment opportunities (such as the maintenance and repair of irrigation facilities, or farm machinery) that have opened up as a result of the Green Revolution (Herdt 1985: 329–51).

In terms of income distribution, early concern that large farmers would benefit more than small farmers from the new technology appear to have been premature. Over a period of time, the rate of adoption of HYVs by large and small farmers have tended to be the same (Herdt 1985: 329–51), and in some studies, income distribution between farmers were observed to have become more, rather than less, equal after HYVs were introduced (Soejono 1976: 80–89).

There is little doubt that the Green Revolution has caused significant environmental damage. The heavy application of chemical fertilisers and pesticides has polluted waterways and made it difficult to sustain some side-line activities, such as the rearing of fish in ponds. In addition, multiple cropping has led to soil exhaustion, which has encouraged even greater use of chemical fertilisers (Bowonder 1981: 293–313).

Regional income disparities have also been aggravated by the Green Revolution. Areas which are well endowed with irrigation facilities, good soils and favourable weather conditions, have been able to reap the benefits of growth of HYVs to much greater extent than other areas which are less well endowed (Karp 1995: 91–2). Note however that the principal causes of regional income disparities are due to government policy and accidents of nature rather than to the Green Revolution *per se*.

In some countries, the Green Revolution has led to a decline in the acreage devoted to, and production of, secondary crops as a result of an increasing concentration on staples such as rice and wheat (Ram

1979). However, this has primarily been caused by government policies which have favoured the growing of rice and wheat.

While the Green Revolution has increased food production significantly in many Asian countries, and staved off the spectre of mass starvation, it has brought in its wake, a number of important economic, social and environmental problems. Some of these can be attributed directly to the new technology, whilst others are more the result of the economic, social and political environment into which the new technology has been introduced.

CONCLUSION

Remarkable changes have occurred in the economies of Asian countries since the end of the Second World War. Starting as predominantly agricultural economies, many Asian countries have made considerable progress toward becoming industrial economies. This is most pronounced in the Asian NICs, and in the ASEAN countries, and least pronounced in the Communist countries of Asia, and in the South Asian subcontinent.

Industrialisation (with few exceptions) began with import-substitution. In the early 1960s, the Asian NICs switched to export-oriented industrialisation, and were followed by China in the late 1970s, and many ASEAN countries in the mid-1980s. Since then, some countries in the former Indochina (especially Vietnam), and in South Asia, have also followed suit.

The shift from import-substituting industrialisation to export-oriented industrialisation was accompanied by a move away from regulated, state-dominated economies, to deregulated, market-oriented economies. This involved dismantling trade barriers, financial market liberalisation, removing distortions in the price system and making labour markets more competitive. However, in areas in which there was little comparative advantage, import barriers were maintained. By the 1980s, many Asian countries had become major world producers and exports of labour-intensive manufactured goods.

Another important aspect of Asian development during the second half of the twentieth century has been the development of agriculture. The introduction of High-Yielding Varieties of rice and wheat raised productivity and food supplies significantly (inspite of a steady decline in the proportion of the labour force engaged in agriculture), and resulted in a Green Revolution in the countryside. However, this has not been without social cost, as the environment has been damaged by the heavy use of chemicals, the output of secondary crops has declined, and regional income disparities have widened. In some regions, unemployment may have been exacerbated by increased mechanisation, and income distribution may have deteriorated. In spite of these negative outcomes, the Green Revolution has fulfilled its main promise, and has helped to avert the widespread food shortages that were feared in the 1950s.

CHAPTER 4

Economic Growth and Development

INTRODUCTION

One of the most important changes that has occurred in Asian countries since the Second World War has been rapid economic growth and development. Starting as poor, less developed countries in the 1950s, with poor prospects for rapid economic advancement, many Asian countries developed rapidly. The Asian NICs were the first to experience an acceleration of growth rates, based on manufactured exports, in the 1960s. They were followed in the late 1970s by China, and in the mid-1980s by ASEAN countries. Countries in South Asia, and some in Southeast Asia (for example, the Philippines), did not begin to share in the rapid economic growth of the region until the 1990s.

With rapid economic growth, many Asian countries experienced rising average incomes and living standards. By the 1980s, Singapore, Hong Kong SAR and Taiwan had been recognised as having achieved developed country status. By the 1990s, South Korea was included in this category, having been admitted into the Organisation for Economic Development and Cooperation (OECD). Meanwhile, China and the ASEAN countries had achieved such high rates of economic growth that they were widely believed to be on the threshold of attaining NIC status.

The remarkable growth and development of the Asian NICs, China and ASEAN countries (accomplished in the relatively short time span of 25 to 30 years) caused many (including the World Bank) to declare their economic performance nothing short of miraculous. This euphoric assessment evaporated in the middle of 1997 when the Asian currency crisis hit the region and plunged many Asian countries into a deep recession. In addition, the costs that the people in these countries had to pay, for achieving rapid economic growth and development, was rapidly becoming appreciated.

FROM ECONOMIC STAGNATION TO RAPID ECONOMIC GROWTH

Economic stagnation in the 1950s

In the decade after the end of the Second World War, most Asian countries experienced low rates of economic growth. The disruption of international trade and the destruction of infrastructure during the war years made it difficult for these countries to achieve high rates of economic growth in the 1950s. The Korean War (1951–53) devastated the (South) Korean economy, although it did provide a boost to economic growth to some countries (such as Singapore and Taiwan), which benefited from the war effort on the Korean peninsula.

In addition, the 1950s were also years of high population growth in many Asian countries. A combination of "pent-up demand" during the war, and inward migration from adjacent countries, resulted in high rates of population growth in many South and Southeast Asian countries.

As a result of these factors, the level and rate of growth of real per capita incomes in many Asian countries during the 1950s were low. Some countries, such as South Korea and Taiwan, were thought by many to have poor prospects for economic advancement. It was well into the 1960s before many countries in the region began to experience rapidly rising growth rates of real per capita incomes. Table 4.1 shows the relevant data. Accurate data for the 1950s are difficult to obtain. The table shows the best estimates that were available. Separate data for Bangladesh were not available as it was then part of Pakistan.

**TABLE 4.1: RATES OF GROWTH OF REAL PER CAPITA GDP
AND POPULATION IN THE 1950S**

Country	Period	Real Per Cap GDP	Population
India	1950–61	1.5	1.7
Pakistan	1950–61	1.7	1.9
Sri Lanka	1950–61	0.9	2.6
Myanmar	1950–61	2.4	1.8
Thailand	1950–61	1.1	2.7
Malaysia	1955–61	2.8	3.0
Singapore	1950–61	5.4	2.8
Indonesia	1950–60	3.6	2.2
Philippines	1950–61	3.7	2.8
Hong Kong	1950–60	7.6	3.4
China	1950–61	3.2	2.2
South Korea	1953–61	1.9	2.6
Taiwan	1950–61	4.0	3.7

Sources: Cheng (1982); Booth (1998); United Nations, *Yearbook of Statistics* (various issues); United Nations, *Demographic Yearbook* (various issues); Ashbrook (1975); Council for Economic Planning and Development, *Taiwan Statistical Data Book* (various issues)

Table 4.1 shows that many Asian countries (especially those in South Asia) experienced low rates of growth (between 1% and 2% per annum) of average incomes during the 1950s, and high rates of growth (between 2% and 3% per annum) of population. Singapore, Indonesia, the Philippines, Hong Kong, Taiwan and China are exceptions. In the case of Singapore and Hong Kong, the recovery in the growth of world trade after the war boosted growth in these countries. Indonesia, the Philippines and Taiwan implemented import-substitution in the 1950s, and experienced high growth as a result of this. South Korea was engulfed in the Korean War during the first half of the decade. China experienced high growth rates during the reconstruction period in the early 1950s, which was followed by the First Five Year Plan (1953–57), during which Soviet-style heavy industrialisation was carried out with the help of the Russians.

Rapid economic growth

Rapid economic growth and development began in Asia in the 1960s when the Asian NICs began to embark on export-oriented industrialisation. By the late 1970s, China began to register accelerating rates of economic growth, when market-oriented economic reforms were implemented. In the mid-1980s, many ASEAN countries began to implement export-oriented industrialisation in earnest, resulting in rapid rates of economic growth in Thailand, Malaysia and Indonesia. They were followed by Vietnam in the late 1980s. By the early 1990s, the economic performance of many countries in Southeast and East Asia had been so impressive that it was regarded by the World Bank as nothing short of a miracle (World Bank 1993). In 1997, the Asian Development Bank predicted that within the next 30 years, many countries in Asia would have caught up with the West in terms of economic development and living standards (Asian Development Bank 1997: 121–128).

THE ASIAN NICS, 1960–2000

The Asian NICs began to implement export-oriented industrialisation in the first half of the 1960s. As a result of this, large flows of foreign capital (in the form of foreign investment or foreign loans), and foreign technology (often brought in by multinational corporations, or licenced from them) flowed into these countries. Together with local sources of finance, these were directed into export-oriented industries which specialised in labour-intensive manufactured goods (such as textiles, clothing and footwear, as well as electronics component assembly). Employment in these labour-intensive industries grew rapidly, raising incomes and living standards.

Table 4.2 shows that growth rates of GDP rose significantly in the 1960s for all the Asian NICs, reaching double-digits in the case of Hong Kong SAR and Taiwan. At these rates of growth, GDP was doubling approximately every seven years in Hong Kong SAR, every eight years in Singapore and South Korea, and every four and half years in Taiwan. These are remarkable rates of economic growth, never before observed in world history.

TABLE 4.2: THE ASIAN NICS — GROWTH RATES OF GDP

Country	1960–70	1970–80	1980–90	1990–00
Hong Kong SAR	10.0	9.2	6.9	4.0
Singapore	8.8	8.3	6.6	7.8
South Korea	8.5	10.1	9.4	5.7
Taiwan	15.5	20.4	12.4	6.4

Sources: World Bank, *World Development Report* (various issues); World Bank, *World Development Indicators* (various issues); Council for Economic Planning and Development, *Taiwan Statistical Data Book* (various issues)

These high rates of economic growth were maintained (in some cases, increased) during 1970–80, in spite of the two oil crises (in 1973 and 1979) which had severe adverse effects on growth and development.

By the 1980s, however, the growth rates of the Asian NICs had begun to slow down, as they began to lose their comparative advantage in labour-intensive manufactured exports due to rising wages and appreciating real exchange rates. This trend has continued into the 1990s. By this time, the growth rates of GDP of the Asian NICs had fallen to between 4% and 8% per annum — still healthy by world standards, but a far cry from the high growth rates of the 1960s and 1970s.

CHINA, 1978–2000

Rising wages in the Asian NICs (and in the case of Hong Kong SAR and Singapore, shortages of space) in the 1980s led to these countries moving their labour-intensive manufacturing industries to other countries where wages were much lower. China was a favourite destination for this purpose, especially for Hong Kong SAR and Taiwan, where geographical proximity and cultural affinity led to large transfers of capital from these countries to the southern provinces of China (Guandong and Fujian). At the same time, the quickening pace of market-oriented reforms in China also led to many multinational companies from Western countries, as well as from Japan starting operations in China in the hope of capturing market shares in the large domestic market. The result of this was rapid economic growth in the Chinese economy, starting first in the southern provinces and later spreading into the interiors. This is illustrated in Figure 4.1 which shows the growth rate of GDP in China from 1978 to 2000.

FIGURE 4.1: CHINA — GROWTH RATE OF GDP

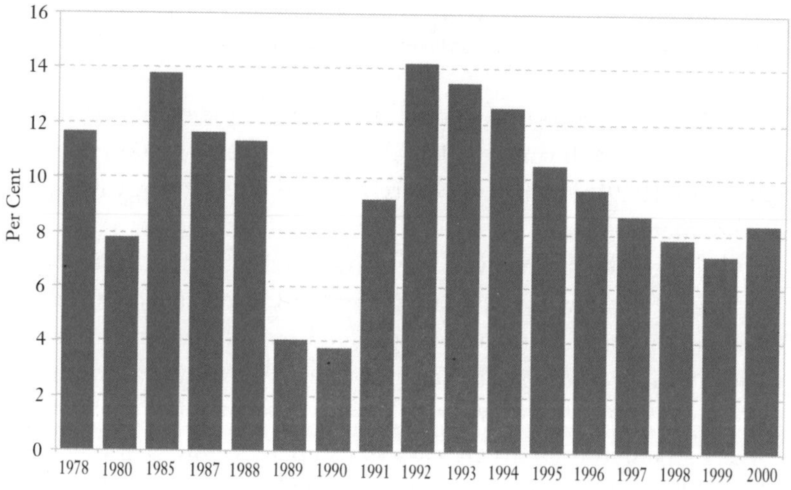

Source: China Statistical Publishing House, *China Statistical Yearbook 2001*

Figure 4.1 shows that for most of the period from 1978 to 2000, China's GDP grew at, or close to, double-digit growth rates, the only exceptions being 1989 and 1990 when the Tiananmen massacre caused a massive reduction in foreign investment flows into China. Note, however, that by the early to mid-1990s, China's rate of economic growth began to decline as the growth of world trade started to slow down, the Japanese economy began to slide into recession, and internal economic problems relating to China's inefficient state-owned industrial sector began to affect its economic performance. Nevertheless, at a growth rate of 8% per annum in 2000, the Chinese economy is still doubling in size every nine years.

ASEAN, 1985–2000

In the early 1980s, oil prices began to decline significantly, and with it, other commodity prices began to decline. This prompted primary product exporting countries in ASEAN to look for other sources of foreign exchange earnings. The sharp and rapid upvaluation of the Japanese yen from 1985, caused a large outflow of foreign investment from Japan in a bid to move relatively less efficient industries to countries where wages and foreign exchange rates were lower. Several ASEAN countries (especially Thailand, Malaysia and Indonesia, but later including Vietnam) benefited from this. The combination of these two factors caused these countries to implement export-oriented industrialisation much more seriously than had previously been the case. The result of this was a significant rise in the rates of economic growth in these countries, especially in the 1990s, when compared to the 1980s. Table 4.3 shows the relevant data.

TABLE 4.3: ASEAN — GROWTH RATES OF GDP

Country	1960–70	1970–80	1980–90	1990–00
Indonesia	3.5	7.2	6.1	4.2
Malaysia	6.5	7.9	5.3	7.0
Philippines	5.1	0.7	1.0	3.3
Thailand	8.2	7.1	7.6	4.2
Cambodia	3.1	NA	NA	4.8
Laos	NA	NA	NA	6.5
Myanmar	2.6	5.0	NA	6.6
Vietnam	NA	NA	4.6	7.9

Sources: World Bank, *World Development Report* (various issues); World Bank, *World Development Indicators 2002*

Table 4.3 shows that in the case of Indonesia, the growth rate of GDP was low during the 1960s. This was primarily due to political turmoil and economic mismanagement in the early 1960s, and violent events leading up to the change of President and government in 1965. The 1970s saw a marked rise in Indonesia's rate of GDP growth, boosted by the sharp rise in oil prices in 1973 and 1979. However, growth slipped in the early 1980s, as the price of oil started to decline markedly. In the late 1980s, Indonesia's rate of GDP growth rose again to 1970 levels, as the country embarked on export-oriented industrialisation, fuelled by large inflows of foreign investment. This was reversed in the late 1990s as a result of the Asian currency crisis.

In the case of Malaysia and Thailand, rates of economic growth in the 1960s and 1970s were high, based on bouyant exports of primary products such as rubber and tin. In the 1980s, Malaysia's growth rate declined sharply as world oil prices fell, but it rose again in the 1990s, as the country moved into export-oriented industrialisation. Thailand did not suffer a fall in its rate of growth in the 1980s as it was not an oil exporter. Its high rates of economic growth in the 1980s mask its change from a primary product exporter to an exporter of labour-intensive manufactured goods. Like Indonesia, it suffered markedly from the Asian currency crisis.

The Philippines experienced high growth rates in the 1950s when it implemented import-substitution, but during 1970-90, suffered low rates of economic growth as a result of internal political instability, poor infrastructure, and a series of natural disasters. Growth rates began to rise in the 1990s as a result of the economic reforms of the Ramos government which brought political, as well as macroeconomic, stability to the country.

In Vietnam, rates of economic growth were moderate in the 1980s, but had been on a downward trend, as the country began to suffer increasingly from the inefficiencies of a Soviet-type centrally-planned economy. Market-oriented reforms in the 1980s resulted in an opening up of the Vietnamese economy to foreign investment and trade, and led to a significant rise in its rate of GDP growth in the 1990s. This is also apparent in the other former Indo-Chinese states as well as in Myanmar.

Other countries in Asia (especially in South Asia, and the Philippines) did not share in this significant improvement in economic performance until the 1990s, primarily because of unfavourable political and economic circumstances. Until the 1990s, many were still implementing import-substitution under tariff protection, and/ or were characterised by internal political instability (in some cases, erupting in open internal warfare).

THE EAST ASIAN MIRACLE

The rapid rate of economic growth of many countries in Southeast and East Asia from the 1960s has transformed these countries from poor, less developed countries into economic powerhouses. Many of these countries have become important centres of world manufacturing and major participants in world trade. This has prompted many to regard their post-war economic performance as miraculous (World Bank 1993). Thirty or forty years ago, few would have thought that countries such as Singapore or Malaysia would one day become major exporters of manufactured goods, or achieve standards of living that are fast approaching those of developed countries.

The euphoria over the East Asian miracle took a crushing blow when the Asian currency crisis hit the region in the middle of 1997, and plunged many Southeast and East Asian countries into deep recessions. Suddenly, what was once considered a miracle, was now pronounced nothing but a mirage. Paragons of successful economic developments were now considered to be the worst examples of economic mismanagement.

With the benefit of hindsight, the extreme optimism that surrounded the pronouncement of the East Asian miracle, was as unjustified as the extreme pessimism that followed the onset of the Asian currency crisis. The spectacular economic performance of Southeast and East Asian countries during the 1960–97 period was not in the miracle class of events. It could be explained in terms of conventional economic analysis (Tan 1995: 93–131). Similarly, the onset and consequences of the Asian currency crisis need not have evoked the deep pessimism that followed it. By early 1998, signs of economic recovery had begun to appear, and by mid-1999, had strengthened to such an extent that the Asian currency crisis had all but been considered over (Sender 1999: 30–32).

THE GROWTH OF EXPORTS

One of the most important facets of the rapid economic growth of Southeast and East Asian countries since the 1960s, is the growth of their exports. Since these exports were generated by export-oriented manufacturing industries, the growth of their total exports was driven by the growth of their manufactured exports. Starting with labour-intensive manufactured exports in the 1960s and 1970s, many of these countries progressed into more capital and skill-intensive manufactured exports by the 1980s and 1990s.

In the process of this rapid economic transformation, the distribution of world manufacturing, and of world manufactured exports changed. By the 1980s, Southeast and East Asian countries had become the major sources of world labour-intensive manufactured exports, and some were fast becoming major sources of world exports of machinery and other capital and skill-intensive products.

Export growth

The implementation of export-oriented industrialisation in many Southeast and East Asian countries resulted in a significant rise in the growth of their exports, especially of manufactured exports. The experience of some selected countries in the region illustrates this. The relevant data are shown in Figure 4.2.

Figure 4.2 shows that in 1970–75, Taiwan (representing the Asian NICs) had the highest rates of growth of manufactured exports. However, by 1985–90, the rate of growth of Taiwan's manufactured exports had declined to 18% per annum, as it began to lose its comparative advantage in labour-intensive manufactured exports. By 1990–2000, Taiwan's manufactured export growth rate had declined to 11% (still respectable, but about a third of what it had been in the 1970–80 period).

By 1985–90, several ASEAN countries had emerged as major exporters of labour-intensive manufactured exports (much of which had been transferred from the Asian NICs). During this period, the rate of growth of manufactured exports was 63% per annum for

Thailand, 33.3% for Indonesia, and 13.7% for Malaysia, far higher than that of the Asian NICs.

FIGURE 4.2: THE GROWTH OF MANUFACTURED EXPORTS

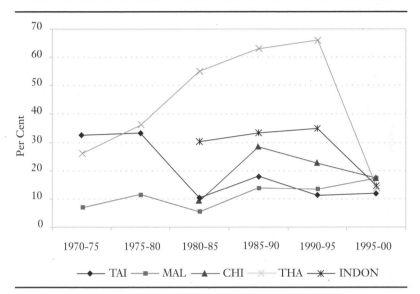

Sources: Ministry of Finance, Malaysia, *Economic Report* (various issues); Bank of Thailand, *Quarterly Bulletin* (various issues); Biro Pusat Statistik, *Expor* (various issues); State Statistical Bureau, *China Statistical Yearbook 2001* (Beijing: China Statistical Publishing House)

From 1980–85 onwards, China had also established itself as a world exporter of labour-intensive manufactured exports (much of it transferred from Hong Kong SAR and Taiwan). During this period, its exports grew by an average of about 30% per annum. By 1990–2000, the rate of growth of China's manufactured exports had averaged 18% per annum, lower than during 1980–85, but still impressive.

By the 1990s, the Asian NICs had moved into specialising in the manufacture of capital and skill-intensive exports, whilst their place in the export of labour-intensive manufactured goods had been taken by some Southeast Asian countries (such as Thailand, Malaysia and

Indonesia), and by China. The growth of Indonesia's and Thailand's manufactured exports fell significantly in 1995–2000 as a result of the Asian currency crisis.

The distribution of world production and exports of manufactured goods

The rapid industrialisation of Southeast and East Asian countries since the 1960s led to a major shift in the distribution of the production of manufactured goods in the world, and in world exports. From the 1960s onwards, the share of Southeast and East Asian countries in world production of manufactured goods, and world exports increased significantly, as a result of the rapid export-oriented industrialisation of the Asian NICs, China, and ASEAN countries.

Table 4.4 shows the share of world manufacturing output accounted for by Southeast and East Asian countries from 1975 (the earliest data available) to 2000. Myanmar's share of world manufacturing output was negligible, and is not shown in the table.

From 1975 to 1995, the share of Southeast and East Asian countries in world manufacturing output rose from 15.7% to 34.5%, largely because of the rapid industrialisation of China. The Asian NICs also increased their share of world manufacturing output significantly, from 2.3% in 1975 to 6.2%. The same is true of the ASEAN countries which increased their share of world manufacturing output from 1.9% in 1975 to 15.7% in 1995. South Asian countries also increased their share of world manufacturing output, but by a smaller magnitude. Their share of world manufacturing output rose from 2.9% in 1975 to 7.5% in 1995. The share of world manufacturing of many Southeast and East Asian countries (especially Hong Kong SAR, Singapore, Thailand, Malaysia and the Philippines) declined substantially during 1995–2000 as a result of the Asian currency crisis and a general weakening of the world economy.

TABLE 4.4: SHARE OF WORLD MANUFACTURING OUTPUT

Country	1975	1980	1985	1990	1995	2000
Bangladesh	0.0017	0.0007	0.0007	0.0005	0.0031	0.0013
India	0.0232	0.0139	0.0149	0.0120	0.0599	0.0114
Pakistan	0.0030	0.0017	0.0019	0.0015	0.0103	0.0015
Sri Lanka	0.0012	0.0003	0.0004	0.0003	0.0020	0.0004
Thailand	0.0047	0.0035	0.0037	0.0056	0.0538	0.0070
Malaysia	0.0028	0.0026	0.0025	0.0019	0.0305	0.0043
Indonesia	0.0053	0.0051	0.0061	0.0057	0.0530	0.0068
Philippines	0.0065	0.0042	0.0034	0.0027	0.0188	0.0030
Vietnam	NA	NA	NA	0.0003	0.0004	0.0009
Hong Kong SAR	0.0028	0.0032	0.0031	0.0030	0.0035	0.0016
Singapore	0.0023	0.0017	0.0018	0.0026	0.0246	0.0039
South Korea	0.0094	0.0092	0.0121	0.0179	0.0185	0.0231
Taiwan	0.0081	0.0076	0.0102	0.0128	0.0153	0.0146
China	0.0858	0.0414	0.0471	0.0288	0.0516	0.0618
Total	0.1569	0.0952	0.1079	0.0954	0.3453	0.1416

Sources: World Bank, *World Development Indicators 2002*; Council for Economic Planning and Development, *Taiwan Statistical Data Book 2002*

By the 1990s, many Southeast and East Asian countries had become some of the world's largest producers (and exporters) of certain manufactured goods. By this time, Hong Kong SAR had become the world's largest manufacturer of watches and clocks, accounting for 45% of world output. Hong Kong SAR had also become the world's second largest exporter of textiles (11% of world exports), while China, South Korea and Taiwan had become the world's fourth, fifth and sixth largest exporters of textiles. In 1990, South Korea, Taiwan, Singapore and Hong Kong SAR were ranked the sixth, eighth, ninth and eleventh largest world producers of electronics products, whilst China was the largest world producer of toys. South Korea was the world's second largest producer of ships after Japan.

Table 4.5 shows the share of world exports accounted for by Southeast and East Asian countries. Their share of world exports increased from 7.4% in 1975 to 19.7% in 2000, an increase of 2.6 times in 20 years. The share of the Asian NICs in world exports rose from 3.1% in 1975 to 11.5% in 2000, while that of ASEAN countries increased from 2.1% to 4.2%. China's share of world exports increased from 1.4% to 3.9% during 1975 to 2000, while that of South Asian countries rose slightly from 0.8% to 1.0% over the same period of time. For many countries in Southeast and East Asia, manufactured goods dominated their total exports. While many countries in Southeast and East Asia (except Myanmar) experienced a significant increase in their share of world exports as a result of their implementation of export-oriented industrialisation, this was not the case for South Asian countries.

Of the world's 25 largest exporters (in terms of total value of exports) in 2000, seven were Southeast and East Asian countries. China was the seventh largest exporter in the world, Hong Kong SAR was the tenth, South Korea was the twelfth, Singapore was the fourteenth, and Taiwan was the fifteenth largest exporter in the world. In 2000, the total exports of Hong Kong SAR were larger than large world exporters such as Belgium, Spain, Sweden and Switzerland. The total exports of South Korea in 2000 were approximately two and a half times that of Australia or Ireland.

Thus, by the 1990s, many countries in Southeast and East Asia had established themselves as major world producers and exporters of manufactured goods.

TABLE 4.5: SHARE OF WORLD EXPORTS

Country	1975	1980	1985	1990	1995	2000
Bangladesh	0.0005	0.0004	0.0006	0.0005	0.0007	0.0010
India	0.0052	0.0046	0.0051	0.0055	0.0064	0.0066
Pakistan	0.0012	0.0014	0.0015	0.0017	0.0017	0.0014
Sri Lanka	0.0007	0.0006	0.0007	0.0006	0.0008	0.0008
Myanmar	0.0002	0.0003	0.0002	0.0001	0.0002	0.0002
Thailand	0.0032	0.0035	0.0040	0.0070	0.0117	0.0108
Malaysia	0.0058	0.0069	0.0086	0.0090	0.0153	0.0154
Indonesia	0.0092	0.0116	0.0104	0.0078	0.0094	0.0098
Philippines	0.0027	0.0030	0.0026	0.0025	0.0036	0.0062

TABLE 4.5: SHARE OF WORLD EXPORTS (cont'd)

Country	1975	1980	1985	1990	1995	2000
Vietnam	0.0001	0.0002	0.0004	0.0007	0.0010	0.0023
Hong Kong SAR	0.0091	0.0105	0.0168	0.0250	0.0359	0.0312
Singapore	0.0080	0.0103	0.0127	0.0161	0.0244	0.0217
South Korea	0.0100	0.0093	0.0169	0.0198	0.0258	0.0271
Taiwan	0.0042	0.0105	0.0171	0.0205	0.0231	0.0233
China	0.0138	0.0096	0.0154	0.0187	0.0307	0.0392
Total	0.0739	0.0825	0.1130	0.1355	0.1905	0.1970

Sources: World Bank, *World Development Indicators 2002*; Council for
Economic Planning and Development, *Taiwan Statistical Data Book 2002*

ECONOMIC AND SOCIAL DEVELOPMENT

The rapid economic growth of many Southeast and East Asian countries since the 1960s has been accompanied by a significant increase in average incomes and living standards. Some of the Asian NICs are now regarded as developed countries, having equalled, or surpassed many Western countries in this respect.

Average incomes

One indication of the economic success of many Southeast and East Asian countries is the extent to which their average incomes have risen relative to the most developed countries in the world. Figure 4.3 shows the relevant data. It plots per capita GNP of selected Asian countries as a percentage of US per capita GNP in 1978, against the same measures in 1997.

Figure 4.3 shows that the Asian NICs have progressed most in terms of average incomes. Their per capita incomes (as a percentage of US per capita incomes) have increased by large margins between 1978 and 2000; Singapore's per capita income increased from 34% to 72% of US per capita income. Hong Kong SAR's per capita income increased from 32% to 75% of US per capita income. South Korea and Taiwan experienced smaller, but nevertheless significant increases in their per capita incomes relative to that of the USA. Between 1978 and 2000, many ASEAN countries experienced a fall in their per capita incomes relative to that of the USA. This was largely due to the severe recession following the Asian currency crisis in 1998. Some South Asian countries also experienced a slight decline in their per capita incomes as a percentage of US per capita income. These are shown, but not identified in the diagram. For example, in 1978, India's per capita income was 1.9% that of USA's per capita income. By 1997, this has fallen to 1.3%. Similarly, Pakistan's per capita income in 1978 was 2.4% that of USA's per capita income. In 1997, this had fallen to 1.7%.

FIGURE 4.3: PER CAPITA GNP (% USA), 1978 AND 2000

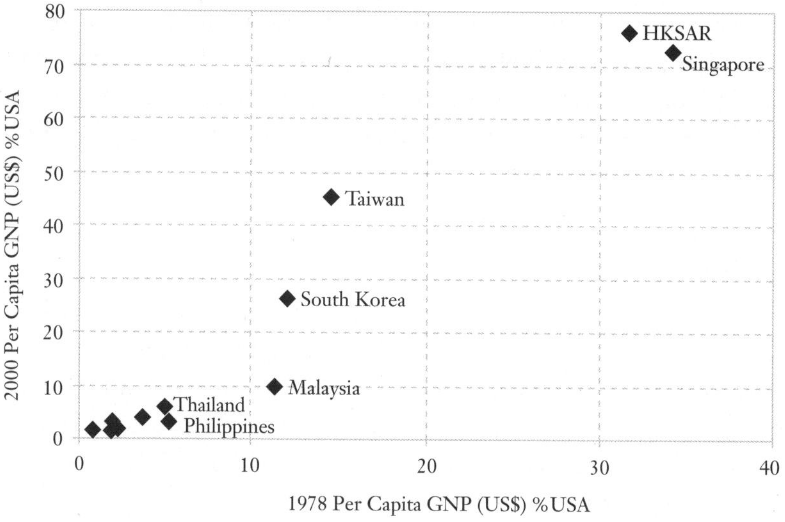

Sources: World Bank, *World Development Report 1981*; World Bank, *World Development Indicators 2002*; Council for Economic Planning and Development, *Taiwan Statistical Data Book 2002*

So, in terms of average incomes, the Asian NICs have progressed the most during the 1978–2000 period. ASEAN countries have not fared well, largely because of the aftermath of the Asian currency crisis. South Asian countries have progressed the least, and in some cases have retrogressed, relative to the USA.

Income distribution

Average incomes, however, do not reveal much about other important aspects of economic development. For example, they do not contain any information about the distribution of income. Increasing average incomes over time could be associated with increasing inequality of income distribution, resulting in a widening gap between the rich and the poor. This could give an impression of rising incomes and living standards for all, when in fact, a relatively small proportion of the population may be benefiting much more from the fruits of economic growth compared to the rest of the population.

In Southeast and East Asia, income distribution improved continuously amongst the Asian NICs during 1960–85 (with the exception of a brief period in the 1970s in South Korea when it deteriorated during a heavy industry development push) (World Bank 1993: 4). During this period, the rapid growth of the Asian NICs was driven by labour-intensive export-oriented industrialisation which resulted in a significant expansion of employment (especially of women). This helped to make the distribution of income more equal. However, since the mid-1980s, labour shortages and rising wages have forced the Asian NICs to shift into capital and skill-intensive industries. This made income distribution in these countries more unequal.

In ASEAN countries, income distribution worsened in Indonesia in the 1970s when the steep increases in oil prices resulted in increased prosperity for some sections of the population and some regions of the country. Since then, a combination of improvements in agriculture (due to the Green Revolution), and export-oriented industrialisation, has resulted in a steady improvement in the distribution of income in Indonesia (Tan 1997: 37–38). In Malaysia, there has not been a consistent pattern of income distribution over time. Income distribution has become more equal during some periods of time, and less equal during other periods of time (often because of government policies). For example, during the mid-1970s, when Malaysia embarked on a heavy industrialisation programme, income distribution worsened, but when it concentrated in labour-intensive export-oriented industrialisation in the mid-1980s, income distribution improved (Tan 1997: 39–40). In the Philippines, income distribution has always been rather unequal (primarily due to the very unequal distribution in the ownership of land and high population growth). Although income distribution has improved over time, the improvement has been marginal, and the inequality of income distribution has remained high (Tan 1997: 40–42). In the case of Thailand, income distribution has been deteriorating steadily over time in spite of rapid economic growth. The main reason for this is the over-concentration of development around the Bangkok area. This has brought prosperity to Bangkok (and the southeast of the country), but left the rest of the country in a sea of poverty (Tan 1997: 43–44).

In China, market-oriented reforms implemented since 1978, has worsened income distribution. Although the Production Responsibility System in agriculture has raised rural incomes relative to urban incomes, this has been offset by increasing income inequality within both the agricultural and urban sectors (Kaye 1993: 46; Economist 1995: S11).

In South Asia, income distribution has always been highly unequal, largely because of the unequal distribution of assets (especially land) and high population growth. Although some progress has been made to reduce inequality in South Asian countries, the degree of inequality of income distribution in these countries remains high (Tan 1999: 192).

The onset of the Asian currency crisis in mid-1997 has worsened income distribution in many countries in Southeast and East Asia. It has plunged millions of people into unemployment and poverty. The extent to which the currency crisis has exacerbated the inequalities of income distribution within countries in the region may have been grossly exaggerated, as not all groups have been as badly hit as others, by the aftermath of the currency crisis (Cameron 1999: 24).

Living standards and basic needs

Another important shortcoming of using average income as a proxy for the level of economic development is that it may not accurately reflect the standard of living, or the adequacy in the provision of basic needs (such as access to a clean water supply, the provision of basic health services, etc.). These physical indicators of development may, however, be examined directly. Table 4.6 shows some of the indicators pertaining to Asian countries.

The data in Table 4.6 broadly confirm that in Figure 4.3. In terms of the selected physical indicators, the Asian NICs have the highest levels of development amongst the countries in the table. In some indices (such as literacy, infant mortality and access to improved water supplies), scores of the Asian NICs are equal, or close, to those of developed countries. ASEAN countries have the second-highest levels of development, with high scores in such indicators as life expectancy, literacy rates, and access to improved water supplies. Amongst ASEAN countries, some interesting exceptions stand out. Socialist countries (such as Myanmar and Vietnam) have high literacy rates in spite of their low levels of per capita income. Life expectancy, literacy rates and infant mortality rates in Brunei approach those of the Asian NICs. This is a reflection of Brunei's very high per capita income. The least developed countries are in South Asia and in the former Indo-Chinese states. In almost every indicator, they score poorly. One exception is Sri Lanka which has high literacy rates and a relatively high number of hospital beds per 1000 of population. Like Vietnam, this is a reflection of years of socialist government policies. China's scores on the various physical indicators of development in the table are in the same range as those of ASEAN countries. One exception is China's high score on hospital beds per thousand people. This is typical of many Communist countries.

**TABLE 4.6: SELECTED PHYSICAL INDICATORS OF
DEVELOPMENT FOR ASIAN COUNTRIES, 2000**

Country	LifeExp	IlitR(M)	InfMort	HBeds	ImpWater	MalNut
Bangladesh	61	48	60	0.3	97	55
India	63	32	69	0.8	88	46
Pakistan	63	43	83	0.7	88	36
Sri Lanka	73	6	15	2.7	83	20
Brunei	76	11	8	NA	NA	NA
Indonesia	66	8	41	0.7	76	42
Malaysia	73	9	8	2.0	89	NA
Philippines	69	5	31	1.1	87	32
Thailand	69	3	28	2.0	80	13
Cambodia	54	20	88	2.1	30	53
Laos	54	36	92	2.6	90	47
Myanmar	56	11	89	0.6	68	42
Vietnam	69	4	27	1.7	56	39
Hong Kong SAR	80	3	3	4.0	NA	NA
Singapore	78	4	3	3.6	100	14
South Korea	73	1	8	5.5	92	NA
Taiwan	75	4	4	5.6	NA	NA
China	67	8	32	2.4	75	14

Key: LifeExp   =   **Life expectancy at birth in years**
        IlitR(M)   =   **Adult male illiteracy rate**
        InfMort   =   **Infant mortality per 1000**
        HBeds   =   **Hospital beds per 1000**
        ImpWater   =   **Access to improved water supplies in % of total
                       population**
        MalNut   =   **Malnutrition (weight for age at under 5 years) in
                       percent, 1993–2000**

**Sources: World Bank, *World Development Indicators 1997* and *2002*; Council for
Economic Planning and Development, *Taiwan Statistical Data Book 2002*;
Ministry of Finance, *Brunei Darussalam Statistical Yearbook 1995***

Human Development Index

The United Nations Development Programme regularly publishes a
Human Development Index (HDI) which combines literacy rates,
life expectancy, infant mortality rates and real per capita incomes (it

is therefore a combination of physical, as well as monetary, indicators of development).

TABLE 4.7: HUMAN DEVELOPMENT INDEX, 1970 AND 2000

Country	1970	2000
Bangladesh	0.174	0.478
India	0.258	0.577
Pakistan	0.226	0.499
Sri Lanka	0.573	0.741
Thailand	0.535	0.762
Malaysia	0.538	0.782
Indonesia	0.316	0.684
Philippines	0.542	0.754
Brunei	NA	0.856
Cambodia	NA	0.543
Laos	NA	0.485
Myanmar	0.384	0.552
Vietnam	NA	0.688
Hong Kong SAR	0.762	0.888
Singapore	0.730	0.885
South Korea	0.589	0.882
Taiwan	NA	NA
China	NA	0.726

Source: United Nations Development Programme, *Human Development Report* (various issues)

Table 4.7 provides additional confirmation of the general pattern of development in Asian countries. The Asian NICs and Brunei had the highest HDI scores (approaching those of developed countries) in 2000, whilst some South Asian countries and some of the former Indo-Chinese states had the lowest HDI scores. ASEAN countries and China had HDI scores in between these two extremes. It is clear from the table that in all countries for which data are available, the level of economic and human development has improved between 1970 and 2000, albeit at different rates. In 2000, Bangladesh's HDI score was only between that of Sri Lanka and Indonesia in 1970.

THE COSTS OF RAPID ECONOMIC GROWTH

During the period 1950–97, rapid economic growth in many countries in Southeast and East Asia was not achieved without significant social and environmental costs. In some countries, low rates of pay, the widespread use of child or convict labour, and poor working conditions prevailed for long periods of time. In other countries, basic human rights were restricted in the name of political and industrial stability. In all countries, considerable damage was inflicted on the environment, as rapid economic growth took priority over almost everything else.

Labour force issues

One of the costs of rapid economic growth in Asian countries has been the exploitation of labour. The use of child labour in South Asian countries (in the manufacture of carpets, sports goods, and other products), the use of convict labour in China, and the use of female labour (many of whom are paid very low wages) in many countries in the region, have attracted much attention. It has been estimated that there are up to 100 million child workers in India (one-third of the children are under 16 years of age), between 12 million and 15 million each in Bangladesh and China, and between 3 million and 5 million each in the Philippines, Thailand and Indonesia. According to the International Labour Office, in Asia, 15% or more of all children between the ages of 10 and 14 years work.

In India and Pakistan, children as young as 8 or 10 years old, are made to work in factories making carpets or sports goods (such as leather footballs). Often, this is the result of their parents being unable to repay their debts. Their children are then made to work in factories making carpets or sports goods, as a way of discharging the debts of their parents. The children themselves are not paid, but are provided with board and lodging (whose cost is deducted from the wages that are used to repay their parents' debts). It has been estimated more than one million children in India, Pakistan and Nepal have been forced to work as modern-day slaves (Fairclough 1996a: 54–57). In China, there have been reports of children being abducted and sold to work in restaurants or as slaves (Gilley 1996: 58).

In cases where the employment of children is not the result of debt repayment, the parents receive the wages (minus costs) that their children earn in the factories in order to supplement their meagre family income. In either case, the children work long hours (12-hour days are common in many factories), and are deprived from obtaining a basic education. Sometimes, the children are held as prisoners for fear that they will run away.

In China, convict labour is widely used in the manufacture of many labour-intensive products. The government considers this a legitimate practice, since it is one way in which those who have been convicted of crimes can repay their debts to society. The convicts themselves do not have a choice as to whether they wish to repay their debts to society in this manner. Developed countries complain that the use of convict labour gives China an unfair competitive advantage in the export of labour-intensive products.

In many Asian countries (such as Malaysia and Indonesia), large numbers of young women are employed in labour-intensive industries (for example, in the manufacture of clothing, shoes, toys, electronic components, and electrical appliances). In the electronics component factories at Bayan Lepas (on the island of Penang), 80% of the workers were young women, and of these, 70% were Malays. They were paid wages that were low (US$0.84 per hour in 1985), compared to similar workers in some neighbouring countries (US$1.58 per hour in Singapore, US$1.33 per hour in Hong Kong SAR). Initially, workers in these factories were not allowed to join national trade unions, but were later allowed to form local, company-specific unions. Although dormitory-accommodation was provided, the social and psychological changes which accompanied the move from rural to factory work was considerable for these young women (Scott 1989:32–34; Greider 1997: 98–100, 397–404).

In many of the more affluent Asian countries, large numbers of migrant workers from poorer surrounding countries have been allowed to take up jobs which the locals no longer want to do. These include construction workers, house maids, and other relatively low-paid occupations. In the late 1980s, some 86,000 Filipinos were working in other Asian countries, while the number of migrant workers in Thailand was about 22,000. Many were paid relatively low wages (a reflection of the nature of the occupations in which migrant workers were employed to do), and cases of gross mistreatment (including physical abuse, rape and even murder), especially of those who worked as house maids, abound (do Rosario and Fairclough 1992: 20–21).

To many observers, the employment of children, convicts, and women, are examples of raw capitalist exploitation which give many Asian countries an unfair competitive advantage compared with manufacturers in developed countries. To others, the employment of children and women, even at pitiful wages, serves a useful social purpose since the alternatives are usually far worse (for example, begging or prostitution). It is also argued that such employment empowers women, by giving them a much higher income than they would otherwise have had, and allowing them to escape from the much harder, and often much lower paid, work in the fields (Scott 1989: 32).

Working conditions

In many Asian countries, workers work long hours for relatively low wages, and under poor working conditions. Unemployment and other work-related welfare benefits (such as medical cover) are either meagre or non-existent, and workplace safety is often a low priority of management. Trade unions are either prohibited, limited to worker welfare (such as the care of aged workers) rather than industrial relations issues, or sometimes, co-opted by governments.

In China, for example, medical cover is often available only as long as a worker is employed, and pensions are paid as long as the worker retires at the normal age of retirement. If a worker is retrenched or sacked, medical cover is terminated, and pensions are no longer paid. This puts considerable hardship on millions of workers who have been sacked from state-owned firms, which have been down-sizing over the last decade or so (Forney 1996: 68–69).

In Shenzhen, near Hong Kong SAR, factory workers earn an average of US$0.12 per hour, working 12-hour days, seven days a week. Workers who are injured in accidents at the workplace (such as fires), often receive no compensation either from the government or from the factories in which they work. Workplace safety regulations, where they exist, are often ignored, leading to many work-related illnesses. Although firms are expected to take out accident and unemployment insurance, few actually take these out (Goldstein and Huus 1994: 35–36).

Poor working conditions are not unique to China, and not limited to locally-owned firms, or firms owned by the more affluent of the Asian countries (Hong Kong SAR, Singapore, South Korea and Taiwan). Even large multinational corporations have been implicated in poor workplace safety issues, often because of the poor practices of their subcontractors. Poorly educated, and insufficiently trained workers have often contributed to the large number of industrial accidents and work-related illnesses that characterise many Asian countries (Saywell 1998: 46–48).

In the more affluent Asian countries (especially in the Asian NICs), working conditions are much better. Child labour is much less prevalent, and worker and employer funded superannuation schemes often provide for the cost of medical treatment. Over time, wages have risen significantly, spurred by increasing labour shortages and occupational health and safety issues have been addressed to a much higher degree than in other Asian countries (Economist 1990: 25–26). In Taiwan, for example, 633,000 persons were covered for medical and injury insurance in 1965. By 1997, this had risen to 9.3 million persons. Between 1976 and 1997, the average monthly hours of work in the manufacturing sector fell from 223 hours to 202 hours, while the average monthly wage rose from NT$4,044 to NT$35,275.

Human rights

Many Asian countries that have achieved high rates of economic growth since the 1960s were governed for long periods of time by military dictatorships (for example, Indonesia, South Korea and Taiwan), or by authoritarian, one-party governments (for example,

Singapore, Malaysia, and Japan). Hong Kong SAR was a colony of Britain until 1997, when it reverted to Chinese rule. Indeed, countries which were more democratic and less authoritarian, tended to be slower growing (for example, India, Thailand and the Philippines).

In many Asian countries, some basic human rights have been proscribed in the interests of political stability and industrial harmony. Freedom of association is often restricted (meetings of more than five persons require a police permit), and freedom of information is frequently curtailed (either by governments banning certain publications deemed to be unfair or subversive, government ownership and control of the media, or by self-censorship on the part of journalists and authors). In some countries (such as Indonesia during the Suharto era), no political parties other than those sanctioned by the government, were allowed. In other countries (for example, Malaysia and Singapore), people could (and can still) be detained indefinitely without trial. As mentioned above, the right to join or form trade unions was frequently prohibited, especially in export-oriented industries, and where unions have been allowed, their functions have been reduced to a subset of their traditional functions (for example, certain welfare activities such as operating discount supermarkets or caring for aged workers).

Environmental damage

Perhaps the most significant cost of rapid economic growth in Asian countries has been environmental damage. Asian countries have one of the worst records of environmental damage in the world. Rapid economic growth has taken precedence over everything else, even though this has resulted in considerable damage to the environment.

Asian cities have one of the worst levels of air pollution in the world. Of the world's 15 most air-polluted cities, 13 are in Asia. The levels of suspended particulate matter (for example, dust and smoke particles) in many Asian cities are two times higher than the world average, and more than five times higher than in developed countries (Asian Development Bank 1997: 201). In an effort to improve the quality of its air as it prepares to host the 2008 Olympics, the Beijing government will spend 10 billion Yuan (US$1.2 billion) to ensure that in three out of every five days, the quality of air will be good or excellent (Chua 2003: A2). Each year, forest fires raging out of control in Indonesia send a thick haze over her neighbouring countries, reaching as far north as the island of Penang (Jayasankaran 1997: 20). In September 1998, ozone gas from industrial activity in southern China descended on Hong Kong, and mixed with fumes from diesel motors, blanketed the city with a deadly smog of nitrogen dioxide (Straits Times 1998: 17). Tail-pipe emissions from motor vehicles in Bangkok have increased the levels of lead in the atmosphere to such high levels that the IQs of children are reduced by six points by the time they reach seven years of age (Fairclough 1996b: 22–24). Much of the air pollution in Asian cities is the result of urban congestion, frantic construction activity, rapid industrial growth, increased power generation based on fossil fuels, and the rapid expansion of the use of motor vehicles, combined with poor, or non-existent, government regulation of polluting activities. The "grow first, clean up later" attitude has been prevalent in many Asian countries.

Asian countries (especially those in Southeast and East Asia) have not fared any better in terms of water pollution. Many rivers in these countries are some of the most polluted in the world. Their levels of suspended solids are four times the world average, and 20 times the levels found in developed countries. Their levels of bacteria from human waste are three times the world average and more than 10 times higher than in developed countries (Asian Development Bank 1997: 203–204). Much of these high levels of water pollution have been caused by the discharge of untreated sewage and industrial effluents as well as the runoff of fertilisers into rivers.

In many Southeast Asian countries, deforestation as a result of logging (both legal and illegal) is a serious problem. Countries in Southeast Asia now have some of the highest rates of deforestation in the world. Between 1981 and 1990, the rate of deforestation was 3.5% per annum in Thailand and the Philippines, 2% per annum in Malaysia, and 1% per annum in Indonesia (Economist 1994a: 29).

Slash and burn agriculture has been a contributing factor as has been the clearing of forests for plantation crops, urban development, and recreational facilities (such as golf courses).

The only country in the region that has taken steps to repair, conserve and improve the environment in significant, and effective ways, is Singapore. Without any prodding from international pressure groups (such as Greenpeace), the Singapore government has limited the use of motor vehicles (through steep user charges), although this was designed primarily to alleviate traffic congestion during peak hours. It has cleaned up the Singapore river which is turned from a dirty, smelly waterway to an attractive tourist attraction. It has transformed Singapore into a green city with the planting of many trees, and has taken measures to limit air pollution from its industries.

With few exceptions, the record of environmental protections in Asian countries has been rather dismal. In the pursuit of rapid economic growth, the needs of future generations have been largely ignored.

CONCLUSION

All countries in Asia have experienced economic growth and development since the 1950s, albeit at varying rates and to varying degrees. Some, such as the Asian NICs, have grown rapidly and are now regarded as having successfully made the transition from less developed, to developed countries. Others, such as the ASEAN countries and China, have also experienced rapid economic growth and rising living standards, and have become major sources of production and exports of manufactured goods. Some countries (especially those in South Asia, and the former Indo-Chinese countries) grew more slowly during the 1950-90 period, but in recent years, have experienced high growth rates.

The Asian currency crisis, which hit the region in mid-1997, caused a severe recession in many Asian countries, and a significant reduction in growth rates in others. Although the worst appears to have passed, and the countries most affected by the crisis have begun to show signs of economic recovery, it will take a few more years before Southeast and East Asian countries can confidently claim to have recovered fully from the Asian currency crisis. These issues will be discussed in greater detail in the next chapter.

In the pursuit of rapid economic growth, most Asian countries have ignored the needs of the environment, or the welfare of future generations. As a result, they have some of the worst records of environmental damage in the world. With few exceptions, the "grow first, clean up later" attitude has prevailed in Asia.

CHAPTER **5**

Links to the Global Economy

INTRODUCTION

One of the most significant developments in Asia, particularly in the last 20 years, has been the increasing integration of many Asian countries into the world economy. By the 1980s, many countries in Southeast and East Asia had opened their doors to international trade, finance, and investment, and by the 1990s, many countries in South Asia were following suit.

The development of satellite communications, electronic transmission of data through computerisation, lower costs of international transport and communications, have all accelerated the process of globalisation, and drawn many Asian countries into the international grid of international trade, finance, and investment. By the 1990s, the idea of a borderless world (Ohmae 1990, 1995) was not just a concept found in books.

While these developments brought economic growth and prosperity to many Asian countries, it has also involved a number of risks. Countries that are wide open to international influences are also highly vulnerable to external shocks. The Asian currency crisis, which hit the region in the middle of 1997, was an example of this.

ASIA IN THE WORLD ECONOMY

International trade

Since colonial times, many Asian countries have been important participants in world trade. Many were (and still are) amongst the world's largest exporters of primary products. Countries such as Malaysia, Indonesia, Thailand and the Philippines have dominated world production and exports of rubber, tin, palm oil, copra, timber, and various spices. Thailand and Vietnam have been important producers and exporters of rice. Thailand is also an important exporter of canned food and cassava (which is used mainly as animal feed in the EU). China is an important exporter of processed food.

Much of the trade of Southeast and East Asia passed through Singapore and Hong Kong SAR, both of which have had over 100 years of experience of trading with the rest of the world.

By the 1980s, the Asian NICs had emerged as important exporters of labour-intensive manufactured goods such as textiles, clothing and footwear, as well as electronic components and toys. By the 1990s, China and the ASEAN countries began to dominate world exports of these labour-intensive manufactured goods, whilst the Asian NICs moved up the "technological ladder" (Tan 1995: 94–100) and started specialising in the exports of consumer durables (such as electrical appliances), machinery, computers and computer peripherals (such as printers and scanners), motor cars, and ships. By this time, many countries in Asia had become prominent in world trade, and were amongst the world's largest exporters. This is shown in Figure 5.1. In 2000, China was the 7th largest exporter in the world followed by Hong Kong SAR in the 10th position, South Korea 12th, Singapore 14th, and Taiwan 15th. Malaysia was the 18th largest exporter in the world, followed by Thailand in the 23rd position. Of the world's largest 25 exporters in 2000, seven were in Asia. This is a reflection of the important role that many Asian countries play in world trade.

The importance of many Asian countries in world trade is also reflected in their trade intensities. One measure of trade intensity is the ratio of total merchandise trade (exports plus imports) to total output (measured by Gross Domestic Product, or GDP). This is shown in Figure 5.2 for the world's largest exports in 2000.

FIGURE 5.1: THE WORLD'S 25 LARGEST EXPORTERS, 2002

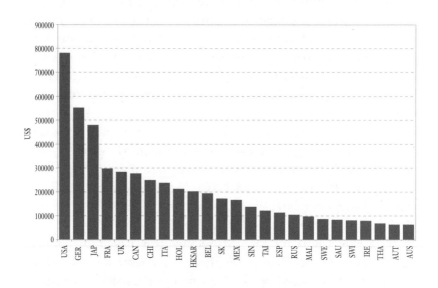

Source: World Bank, *World Development Indicators 2002*

FIGURE 5.2: TRADE INTENSITIES, 2000

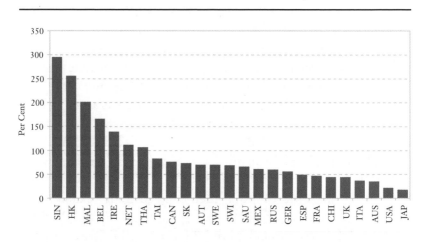

Source: World Bank, *World Development Indicators 2002*

Figure 5.2 shows that, amongst the world's 25 largest exporters in 2000, Asian countries had some of the highest trade intensities. Of the 20 countries with the highest trade intensities in the world, seven were in Asia. Singapore and Hong Kong SAR have very high trade intensities partly because of their very small size. However, Switzerland has approximately the same population as Hong Kong SAR, but its trade intensity is only a quarter of that of Hong Kong SAR. Similarly, Ireland has about the same population as Singapore, but the latter's trade intensity is more than twice as large as the former's.

There are some Asian countries which have low trade intensities. These are mainly in South Asia and in the former Indo-Chinese states. For example, in 2000, India and Pakistan had trade intensities between 20% and 33%, while the figure for Bangladesh was 31%. Until recently, many of these countries closed their doors to international trade, finance and investment.

Another indicator of the degree of openness of countries to international trade is the extent to which they impose tariffs (taxes) in imports. Table 5.1 shows the average rate of tariff protection for selected Asian countries in 1990 and 2000, for which data were available.

TABLE 5.1: AVERAGE RATE OF TARIFF PROTECTION, 1990 AND 2000

Country	1990	2000
Bangladesh	114.0	21.3
India	82.0	32.5
Sri Lanka	28.0	9.9
Indonesia	21.0	8.4
Malaysia	17.0	9.3
Philippines	28.0	7.6
Thailand	40.0	16.6
Singapore	0.5	0.0
South Korea	13.3	8.6
China	39.9	16.3

Source: World Bank, *World Development Indicators 1999, 2002*

Table 5.1 shows that, in 2000, many countries included in the table had moderate to low average rates of tariff protection (between 8% and 10%). China, Thailand, and Bangladesh had higher average rates of tariff protection, whilst India had the highest average rate of tariff protection. At the other end of the spectrum is Singapore with one of the lowest average rates of tariff protection in the world. Data was not available for Hong Kong SAR, but it is known that apart from low tariffs on three commodities (alcoholic beverages, tobacco and some petroleum products), no tariffs are imposed on imported goods (Cheng 1982: 168). For all intents and purposes, Singapore and Hong Kong SAR are free-trade economies.

No data were available for the former Indo-Chinese states. However, since the late 1980s, many of these countries have been reducing their tariffs, and opening their economies up to international trade and investment. Although Myanmar's average tariff rate is reasonably low (compared to the rest of ASEAN), quantitative restrictions pose serious obstacles to trade. In 1993, Cambodia's tariff system was revised into four bands, with consumer goods imports facing a maximum tariff rate of 35% to 50%. In Laos, maximum tariff rates have been reduced to 40% (from 80%), and the number of tariff bands has been reduced to six (from twelve). Most import quotas have also been abolished. At the end of 1996, Vietnam's average rate of tariff protection was about 23%. About half of all of Vietnam's tariff lines were in the 0% to 5% range (East Asia Analytical Unit 1997: 318–19).

Private foreign investment

The growing integration of many Southeast and East Asian countries into the world economy is also reflected in their roles in international finance. Many countries in the region are major recipients of private foreign investment (which constitutes a significant proportion of their total investment, or output), and some are now important exporters of capital. In 1998, three of the ten largest recipients of private foreign investment in the world were Asian countries (China 28.0% of the total, Malaysia 3.7%, and Thailand 3.2%).

TABLE 5.2: PRIVATE FOREIGN INVESTMENT, 1997 AND 2000

Country	%GDI 1997	%GDI 2000	%GDP 1997	%GDP 2000
Bangladesh	1.6	2.6	0.3	0.6
India	3.7	2.1	0.9	0.6
Pakistan	7.6	3.2	1.2	0.5
Sri Lanka	11.7	3.8	2.8	1.1
Indonesia	7.0	-16.6	2.2	-4.2
Malaysia	12.1	7.2	5.2	2.0
Philippines	6.0	15.2	1.5	2.8
Thailand	7.0	12.2	2.4	2.8
Cambodia	41.4	26.3	6.7	3.9
Laos	17.9	20.6	5.1	5.4
Myanmar	NA	NA	NA	NA
Vietnam	25.0	15.1	7.2	4.1
Hong Kong SAR	NA	NA	NA	89.2
Singapore	24.0	22.1	9.0	11.6
South Korea	1.8	7.1	0.6	3.2
Taiwan	NA	NA	NA	NA
China	12.8	9.5	4.9	4.3

Sources: World Bank, *World Development Indicators 1999, 2002*; Asian Development Bank, *Key Indicators for Developing Asian and Pacific Countries 1999, 2002*

Table 5.2 shows the ratio of private foreign investment to Gross Domestic Investment (GDI), and to Gross Domestic Product (GDP) in 1997 and 2000. Before the Asian currency crisis (which occurred in 1997), private foreign investment was a significant proportion of GDI and GDP in many Southeast and East Asian countries especially the Asian NICs (except South Korea), China, Sri Lanka, Malaysia, and the former Indo-Chinese states. Much of this has taken the form of multinational corporations establishing production facilities in these countries. In South Korea, inward private foreign investment has been discouraged for many years, but foreign capital entered the country in large quantities in the form of foreign loans. In South Asia, Bangladesh and India stand out as countries in which private foreign investment plays a minimal role in their respective economies, largely because of unfavourable government policies. By contrast, private foreign investment plays a very significant role (especially since the early 1990s) in the economies of many of the former Indo-Chinese states (except Myanmar, which is still regarded by many countries as a pariah state). This is a reflection of their shift away from centrally-planned to market-oriented economies, and their increasing openness to foreign investment. Table 5.2 shows that following the Asian currency crisis, foreign investment in many Asian countries fell, especially in ASEAN countries (Indonesia stands out in this regard), as foreign investors shied away from the region.

Since the late 1980s, the Asian NICs have become important exporters of capital. Faced with rapidly increasing wages at home, many of these countries moved their labour-intensive industries to other Asian countries (especially China, the ASEAN countries, and Vietnam) in search of lower costs. The principal mechanism which facilitated this transfer of production was foreign investment. Much of the private foreign investment in China comes from Hong Kong SAR and Taiwan (Tan 1995: 285–288), while in countries like Malaysia and Indonesia, foreign investment from Singapore and the other Asian NICs are a significant proportion of the total inflow of foreign investment (Tan 1995: 94–100).

International finance

Another aspect of the internationalisation of Southeast and East Asian countries is in the realm of international finance. Some countries such as Singapore and Hong Kong SAR, are now important regional financial markets.

By the early 1990s, average daily turnover in foreign exchange markets in Singapore and Hong Kong SAR was about US$70 billion, the same volume as Zurich, and higher than that of Sydney, or Paris. By 2000, Singapore and Hong Kong SAR were amongst the world's five largest foreign exchange markets in terms of average daily turnover. By then, Singapore and Hong Kong SAR accounted for about 10% each of total currency quotations in the world, a higher share than Tokyo, Zurich, Sydney or Paris.

Both Singapore and Hong Kong SAR are important centres of international banking and finance. Of the 500 largest banks in Asia in the mid-1990s, 25 were located in Hong Kong SAR, and 11 were located in Singapore. Banks in Singapore and Hong Kong SAR are some of the strongest and best managed and supervised in the world. Their capital-adequacy ratios are around 20%, far higher than that required by their central banks (about 8%), or by the Bank of International Settlements (about 12%). The four Asian NICs accounted for nearly 20% of the largest 500 banks in Asia, whilst the ASEAN countries (excluding Singapore) accounted for another 27%.

Another indication of the importance of Asian countries in international finance is the relative size of their stock markets. Table 5.3 shows the relevant data for those countries for which data was available.

TABLE 5.3: ASIAN STOCK MARKETS, 1995 AND 2001

Country	SMCap 1995	SMCap 2001	SM/GDP 1995	SM/GDP 2001
Hong Kong SAR	303705	623398	211.4	383.3
China	42055	523952	6.0	53.8
South Korea	181955	220046	39.9	32.5
Singapore	148004	152827	176.8	165.7
Malaysia	222729	120007	261.1	130.4
India	127199	110396	39.2	32.4
Philippines	58859	41523	79.3	69.0
Thailand	141507	36340	84.7	24.1
Indonesia	66585	23006	33.6	17.5
Pakistan	9286	4944	15.3	10.7
Sri Lanka	1998	1332	15.5	6.6
Bangladesh	1323	1145	4.5	2.5

Key: SMCap = Stock Market Capitalisation (US$ Million)
      SM/GDP = Stock Market Capitalisation (% GDP)
Source: World Bank, *World Development Indicators 1997, 2002*

Table 5.3 shows that in terms of stock market capitalisation in 1995, Hong Kong SAR had the largest stock market in Asia, followed by Malaysia, South Korea, Singapore, Thailand and India. Hong Kong SAR's stock market was about the same size as that of Canada (US$ 336,344 million) and the Netherlands (US$356,481 million), but was larger than that of many developed countries such as Australia (US$245,218 million), Italy (US$209,522 million), Spain (US$197,788 million) and Sweden (US$178,049 million). Furthermore, in Hong Kong SAR, Malaysia, Singapore, Thailand, and the Philippines, stock market capitalisation was a significant proportion of GDP. This is a reflection of the importance of the stock market and share trading in these economies. Although the stock market in some of these countries is closed to foreigners, financial market deregulation in the 1990s has resulted in a gradual opening up of these stock markets to foreign investors. The countries at the bottom of the table (China, Pakistan, Sri Lanka and Bangladesh) had relatively small stock markets, reflecting the early stages of their integration in world financial markets.

Table 5.3 also shows how the Asian currency crisis wreaked havoc on the stock markets of some ASEAN countries. In Malaysia, Thailand, Indonesia and the Philippines, stock market capitalisation in 2001 declined (very significantly in some cases, for example, Thailand, Indonesia and Malaysia) as investors dumped their shares. With the exceptions of Hong Kong SAR and China, the ratio of stock market capitalisation to GDP fell (in some cases, for example, Malaysia, Thailand and Indonesia, by large amounts).

Perhaps one of the most important indicators of the importance of Asian countries in international finance is their participation in world financial flows, especially direct and portfolio foreign investment. As pointed out above, in the 1970s and 1980s, large flows of direct foreign investment entered many countries in Southeast and East Asia. However, in the mid-1980s and early 1990s, many of these countries were large recipients of portfolio foreign investment and foreign loans. Although these financial flows accelerated economic growth rates in the 1970s and 1980s, they eventually led to the Asian currency crisis, which will be discussed at the end of this chapter.

The rising importance of foreign portfolio investment in many Asian countries can be illustrated by the case of Thailand since 1980. Figure 5.3 shows the relevant data. As the figure shows, foreign direct investment started rising significantly after 1985 as a result of the upvaluation of the yen (much of the foreign direct investment in Thailand during this period was from Japan). However, by the early 1990s, the Japanese economy was in trouble and Japanese foreign investment started to decline. By this time, foreign portfolio investment in Thailand had started to rise steeply, reaching over US$4 billion in 1993 and 1995. By the early 1990s, foreign portfolio investment in Thailand was more than twice that of foreign direct investment. Short-term external private debt rose from US$2.3 billion in 1980 to US$29.2 billion in 1996. A similar pattern was obtained in many other Southeast Asian countries, especially Malaysia and Indonesia. By the mid-1990s, foreign portfolio investment (most of it in short-term maturities) had become large relative to foreign reserves in many countries in the region. This ranged from 167% in Indonesia to 25% in Malaysia.

With the rapid increase in the use of computers in financial market operations, as well as large increases in pension and other funds in developed countries, all looking for profitable investments, many countries in Southeast and East Asia became the flavour of the month with fund managers who poured massive amounts of portfolio investment funds in these countries. They were not to be outdone by foreign banks which extended large foreign loans. Thus, by the mid-1990s, many countries in the region had become major players in international financial markets. As will be explained later, this made them very vulnerable to the volatility of international financial markets, and led to catastrophic consequences when the Asian currency crisis erupted in 1998.

FIGURE 5.3: FOREIGN INVESTMENT IN THAILAND

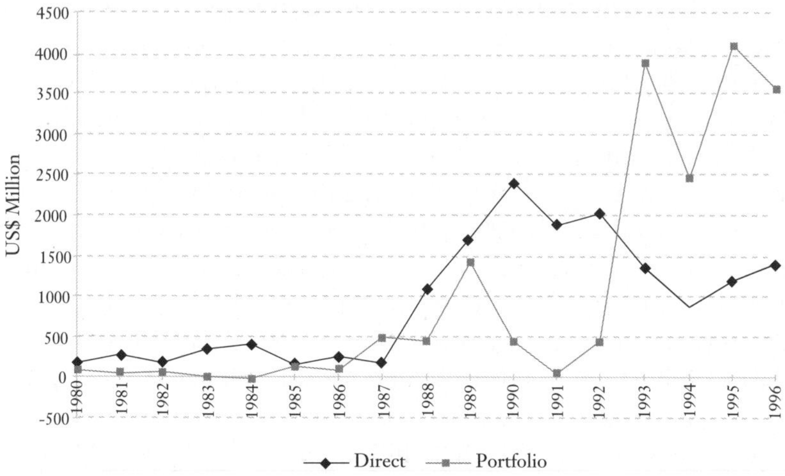

Source: Bank of Thailand, *Quarterly Review* (various issues)

THE DOMINANCE OF THE USA,
EU, JAPAN AND CHINA

Global linkages have been dominated by the large trading nations of the world, especially USA, EU and Japan. In recent years, they have been joined by China, which is destined to become the largest economy in the world in the first decade of the 21st century.

International trade and investment are dominated by USA, EU and Japan. In 1997, USA accounted for 14.4% of world trade, the EU accounted for 37.4%, and Japan accounted for 7.1% of world trade. Many countries in Asia are highly dependent on USA, EU and Japan as markets for their exports. This is shown in Table 5.4.

The table shows that most South Asian countries depend much more on USA and EU (rather than on Japan) as markets for their exports. Most ASEAN countries send between 13% and 19% of their exports to USA. However, the importance of Japan to Indonesia, and USA to the Philippines, should be noted. With the exception of Vietnam, and possibly Laos, the former Indo-Chinese

86

states do not send very much of their exports to USA, EU or Japan. Laos's dependence on the EU, and Vietnam's dependence on the EU and Japan are exceptions to this. For obvious historical reasons, the former Indo-Chinese states do not trade very much with USA. The Asian NICs are much more dependent on USA and the EU for the exports than on Japan. Historically, the Japanese economy has been relatively closed to imports, and much of the output of Japanese firms located in the Asian NICs, export their products to USA and the EU. China, on the other hand, is dependent on USA, EU and Japan for her export markets.

TABLE 5.4: SHARE OF TOTAL EXPORTS (IN PER CENT), 1996

Country	USA	EU	Japan
Bangladesh	31.0	45.0	3.1
India	17.3	29.4	7.4
Pakistan	16.7	30.1	6.5
Sri Lanka	34.1	34.4	6.2
Indonesia	16.5	18.3	28.8
Malaysia	18.2	14.8	13.4
Philippines	32.6	18.6	17.1
Thailand	18.0	15.7	16.8
Cambodia	1.2	14.0	1.8
Laos	4.8	27.0	6.6
Myanmar	8.3	6.3	7.4
Vietnam	4.5	25.0	26.4
Hong Kong SAR	21.1	15.8	6.5
Singapore	18.4	13.4	8.2
South Korea	16.8	13.3	12.3
Taiwan	23.2	14.6	11.8
China	17.7	15.0	20.4

Sources: Asian Development Bank, *Asian Development Outlook 1996*; Council for Economic Planning and Development, *Taiwan Statistical Data Book 1998*

In terms of foreign direct investment, USA accounted for 39.9% of all foreign direct investment (US$103.6 billion) in the world in 1997. The EU accounted for 45.5%, while Japan accounted for 14.6%. In the same year, USA accounted for 43.3% of total foreign portfolio investment (US$84.6 billion) in the world, the EU accounted for 45.4%, and Japan accounted for 6.4%. Thus, USA, EU and Japan dominate world private financial flows. They also dominate world flows of foreign aid to poor countries.

Since the late 1980s, many of the Asian NICs have become important markets for the exports of other countries, and also as important sources of foreign investment. With rapid economic development and rising average incomes, these countries have become important destinations for the exports of other countries. In addition, the rising balance of payments surpluses of many of the Asian NICs have also made them important sources of foreign investment in many countries.

In many countries in Asia, large proportions of foreign investment are accounted for by USA, EU and Japan. For example, 18.9% of total foreign direct investment in Thailand in 1996 came from USA. The EU accounted for 7.2% and Japan accounted for 23.0%. The Asian NICs accounted for 28.7% of total foreign direct investment in Thailand in 1996. In the same year, USA accounted for 20.4% of total foreign portfolio investment in Thailand. The EU accounted for 8.8%, and Japan accounted for 26.6%. The Asian NICs accounted for 22.8% of total foreign portfolio investment in Thailand in 1996. A similar pattern can be observed for many other Asian countries.

Thus, in respect of international trade and financial flows, USA, EU and Japan dominate world markets. This is not surprising since these are amongst the wealthiest countries in the world, and are therefore expected to be, not only major export markets for many developing countries, but also major sources of international finance. Since the late 1980s, the Asian NICs have also become important sources of foreign direct and portfolio investment for many countries in the region. This is a reflection of the extent to which they have succeeded in transforming themselves from less developed to developed countries.

THE RISKS OF GLOBALISATION

Globalisation can confer many benefits to countries which have forged links with the world economy, but it also involves many risks. World markets, whether for goods or finance, can be very unstable and the economic prosperity that they bring can vanish suddenly.

In international trade, export markets can suddenly disappear if export destinations experience an unexpected economic downturn, or if consumer demand suddenly plummets. Prices of exports can fall significantly because of global oversupply. This applies not only to primary product exports, but also to manufactured goods. An example of the latter occurred in the 1990s, when the price of computer equipment fell by 40% between 1990 and 1997 as a result of world excess supply of computer chips. In 1995, the price of electronic equipment (of all kinds) was 10% above its 1990 level, but by 1997 had fallen to nearly 30% below this level.

In international finance, short-term foreign portfolio investment funds can be withdrawn within a short space of time, plunging host economies into financial crisis. This is what happened during the Asian currency crisis in mid-1997. A loss of confidence in the values of regional currencies led to a massive flight of short-term capital, leaving many regional economies in ruins. The case of Thailand is an excellent example of this. Between 1993 and 1995, foreign portfolio investment and foreign loans increased from 242 billion baht to 490 billion baht, falling to 310 billion baht in 1996. After the Asian currency crisis hit in July 1997, foreign portfolio investment and foreign loans to Thailand were -251 billion baht in 1997, -310 billion baht in 1998 and -291 billion baht in 1998. So, within a few years, a foreign capital inflow of approximately 300 billion baht was reversed into a foreign capital outflow of about -300 billion baht. The consequences for Thailand, its economy and its people, were catastrophic.

In the view of some authors, there is something inherent in the logic of world trade and financial markets that leads to periodic global oversupply and economic instability (Greider 1997: 444–73; Davidson and Rees-Mogg 1994: 338–65). Countries that have forged close links with the global economy cannot escape the consequeces of its inherent instability. While globalisation can confer great wealth and prosperity to nations, it can also reduce them to ashes.

THE ASIAN CURRENCY CRISIS

The Asian currency crisis is the most recent example of the risks of globalisation. Many countries in Southeast and East Asia which had experienced spectacular growth rates in the 1980s, financed primarily by short-term foreign portfolio investment and foreign loans, were reduced to poverty when these funds were suddenly withdrawn in the latter half of 1997. A detailed analysis of the causes and consequences of the Asian currency crisis is beyond the scope of this book. A brief introduction to this topic is given below. A comprehensive discussion of the Asian currency crisis can be found in Tan (2000).

The Asian currency crisis began in Thailand. Between 1985 and 1996, the Thai economy was growing at an average rate of 7% per annum (very high by international standards). As pointed out above, much of this was increasingly being financed by short-term private foreign portfolio investment, and short-term foreign loans (with maturities of less than one year). The massive inflows of these short-term funds (encouraged by the Thai government's deregulation of the banking and finance industry, and the establishment of the Bangkok International Banking Facility, or BIBF) enabled the Thais to invest much more than they saved, and import much more than they exported. By 1995, Thailand's Gross Domestic Investment was 43% of its GDP, while its Gross Domestic Saving was only 36% of GDP. Thailand's trade balance (exports minus imports) was -US$14 billion in 1995, or 8.6% of its GDP (very high by international standards). At the same time, its foreign debt was US$57 billion or 34% of its GDP, and 78% of this debt was in short-term maturities.

The problem for Thailand lay in the fact that it had pegged the value of its currency, the baht to the US dollar (at a rate of 26 baht to one US dollar). With mounting trade deficits, many foreign investors began to fear that Thailand would not be able to maintain the pegged exchange rate of the baht, and would be forced to devalue its currency.

To make matters worse, much of the short-term foreign investment entering Thailand in the early 1990s was going into speculative investments in the property and stock markets (rather than into export-oriented industries which earned foreign exchange). The large inflows of foreign funds contributed to a significant increase in the growth of the money supply, fuelling the demand for, and raising the prices of, property and shares. The stage had been set for a number of important triggers which eventually led to financial panic that set off the Asian currency crisis.

In the middle of 1996, the Bangkok Bank of Commerce (BBC) collapsed amidst a mountain of debt, caused largely because of the fraudulent behaviour of some of its senior executives. This was a warning sign of the fact that the Thai banking and its finance industry was not only weak, but also poorly supervised by the central bank. By the end of 1996, Thailand's manufactured export growth had plummeted to -0.05% (compared to a 20% growth rate in 1995). This was caused primarily by a slowdown in the world electronics market. In early 1997, one of the largest property developers in Thailand, Samprasong Land defaulted on repayments on a US$3.1 billion foreign loan, while another large property developer, Bangkok Land, had accumulated debts equal to 167% of its equity base. These were early warning signs that the property asset bubble was about to burst, as chronic oversupply began to push prices and rentals down. About the same time, Finance One, one of Thailand's largest finance companies, announced that it was in deep financial trouble, with debts of nearly US$7 billion (many finance companies had large exposures to the property market).

The spate of bad financial news early in 1997 led to heavy selling on the Bangkok Stock Exchange, driving share prices down. In addition, speculative attacks on the baht took place as rumours of an imminent devaluation of the currency began to circulate. The central bank, the Bank of Thailand, defended the baht in international financial markets, eventually spending US$20 billion (about half Thailand's total foreign reserves) in the process. The government of Prime Minister Chavalit Yongchaiyud promised publicly not to devalue the baht. As it turned out, this promise was not to be kept.

On July 2, 1997, at 8.30 am, the Bank of Thailand announced that it was no longer going to support the value of the baht and that the currency would be allowed to float immediately. As soon as that announcement was made, the baht went into free fall, depreciating by 17% in a single day. At the same time, the Bangkok Stock Exchange index also started to melt down as investors dumped their shares. The Asian currency crisis had begun.

Almost immediately, the financial panic which had engulfed Thailand spread to other ASEAN countries, especially Indonesia and Malaysia, since these too had suffered from many of the economic problems that had afflicted Thailand. Other countries which had much stronger economic fundamentals and much more robust banking and financial system (such as Singapore and Hong Kong SAR), were also affected adversely (albeit to a less severe degree), only because they were located in the region, and could not insulate themselves from the "contagion effects" of the currency crisis.

The extent of the devastation caused by the Asian currency crisis can be seen from Figures 5.4 and 5.5.

FIGURE 5.4: FOREIGN EXCHANGE RATES OF ASEAN COUNTRIES (JAN 1997=100)

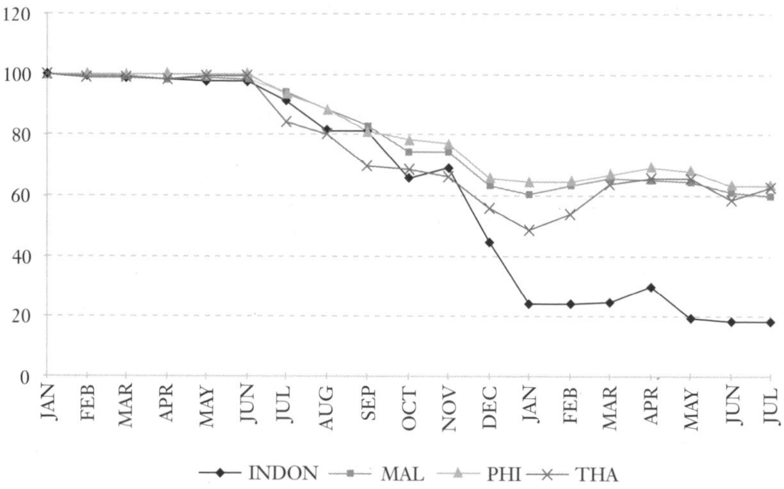

Source: *Far Eastern Economic Review* (various issues)

**FIGURE 5.5: FOREIGN EXCHANGE RATES
OF THE ASIAN NICS (JAN 1997=100)**

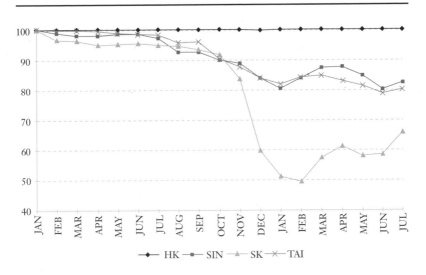

Source: Same as Figure 5.4

Figure 5.4 shows that by January 1998, the Indonesian rupiah had lost about 80% of its value relative to the US dollar, compared to January 1997. The Thai baht had lost about 50% of its value, while the other ASEAN currencies (the Malaysian ringgit and the Philippine peso) had each lost about 40% of their values.

Figure 5.5 shows that by January 1998, the South Korean won had lost 50% of its value relative to the US dollar, compared to January 1997. The Singapore and Taiwanese dollars had lost about 20% of their values, whilst the Hong Kong SAR dollar retained its currency peg to the US dollar.

The meltdown of Southeast and East Asian stock markets is shown in Figures 5.6 and 5.7.

FIGURE 5.6: ASEAN STOCK EXCHANGE INDEXES (JAN 1997=100)

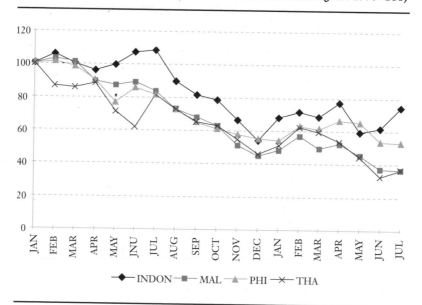

Source: Same as Figure 5.4

FIGURE 5.7: ASIAN NICS' STOCK EXCHANGE INDEXES (JAN 1997=100)

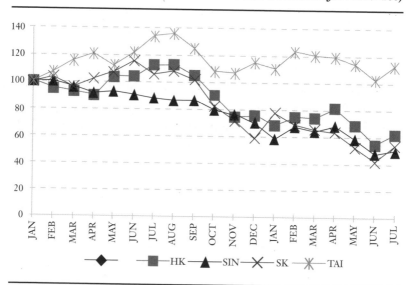

Source: Same as Figure 5.4

Figure 5.6 shows that by July 1998, the Malaysian and Thai stock markets had lost about 60% of their value, relative to January 1997. The Philippines and Indonesian stock markets had lost about 40% of their value.

In the Asian NICs, stock markets in Singapore, South Korea and Hong Kong SAR had lost between 40% and 60% of their value, compared to January 1997. The Taiwanese stock market remained virtually unscathed by the Asian currency crisis.

Thus, within a year, the financial panic that had started in Thailand in July 1997, had spread to most countries in Southeast and East Asia, causing massive depreciations of regional currencies, and the largest destruction of financial wealth in world history. The human and other costs of the crisis were staggering, as millions of people were plunged into poverty. The fruits of decades of successful development were wiped out almost overnight. This was a very painful lesson on the risks of globalisation that the countries of Southeast and East Asia had to learn.

CONCLUSION

One of the most important developments in Asia during the second half of the 20th century has been the links that countries in the region have forged with the global economy. Many of the countries in Southeast and East Asia have become important participants in world trade, foreign investment and international finance, and important success stories in world development.

The dominance of USA, EU, and Japan in world economic affairs has been very significant. Many countries in Asia depend on these countries, either as markets for their exports, or as sources of capital and technology. Only some countries in the former Indo-Chinese states (as well as in South Asia) do not share this heavy dependence on USA, EU and Japan.

Although globalisation can confer many economic benefits, it can also impose high costs on countries which are integrated into the world economic and financial system. Export markets could vanish suddenly, and foreign funds could be withdrawn at very short notice.

This was painfully illustrated in the middle of 1997 when the Asian currency crisis hit the region. Within a few months, countries which had been booming for many years previously, were reduced to poverty. The results of decades of rapid economic growth were wiped out almost overnight. Regional currencies depreciated by very large amounts, and the greatest destruction of financial wealth took place as regional stock markets imploded.

PART **2**

Social Change

6

Demographic Trends

INTRODUCTION

One of the most important changes in Asian countries since the Second World War has been in the area of population growth. Starting with high population growth rates after the war, many countries in the region began to experience a steady decline in fertility and a reduction in population growth. This was most prominent (with few exceptions) in Southeast and East Asia. In South Asia, population growth rates remained higher, although a general decline in the growth of population was also evident there.

In some countries, coercive methods were used to accelerate the decline in the growth of population. A variety of financial and non-financial incentives were used to persuade couples to have fewer children. In other countries, non-coercive methods were used to achieve the same result.

By the 1980s, some countries in the region were beginning to experience labour shortages, and had started to import (or tolerate) migrant labour from neighbouring countries.

One important outcome of declining population growth rates in many Asian countries has been an acceleration in the ageing of the population. With fewer children born each year, and life expectancy increasing, the proportion of retired and elderly people in the total population has risen significantly in many Asian countries. This presents significant challenges to governments in terms of the provision of medical and other facilities for the aged.

DECLINING FERTILITY

In the 1950s, there was considerable concern over rapid population growth in many Asian countries. Total fertility rates of six or more were not uncommon. Crude birth rates of over 40 per thousand were often coupled with crude death rates of under 30 per thousand (in Bangladesh, for example, the crude birth rate in 1960 was 51 per thousand, while the crude death rate was only 25 per thousand). Population growth rates of 3% or more were experienced in many countries. This was underlined by the fact that in many of these countries, the absolute size of population was already large (India, Indonesia and China come to mind). Even a moderate rate of growth of population in these countries would mean large absolute increases in population size. The spectre of a population explosion, large-scale unemployment, and widespread famine cast its shadow over many of these countries.

From the late 1960s, however, population growth rates in many Asian countries began to fall. In most countries in Southeast and East Asia, the decline was rapid and pronounced. In South Asia, the decline was slower and less dramatic. Figure 6.1 shows the relevant data for a selected group of countries.

FIGURE 6.1: POPULATION GROWTH RATES

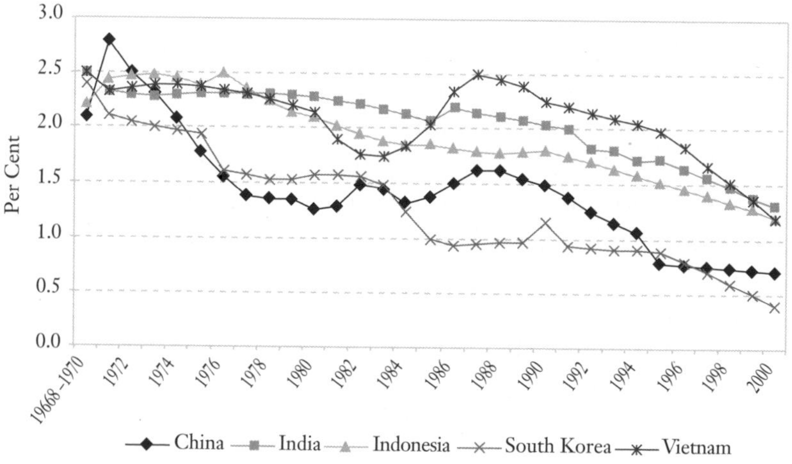

Source: World Bank, *World Development Report* (various issues); World Bank, *World Development Indicators 2002*

Figure 6.1 shows that population growth rates in all the countries included in the graph fell steadily between 1960 and 2000. The decline was most pronounced in East Asia, and is illustrated by the case of South Korea. From a population growth rate of nearly 2.5% per annum in the 1960s, South Korea's rate of population growth declined to less than 1% per annum by the 1980s. A similar pattern can be seen in the case of China (whose population growth rate in the 1960s was affected by the great famine which followed the Great Leap Forward during 1958–61).

In Southeast Asia, population growth rates have also declined over time, but not to the same extent as in East Asia. The data for Indonesia illustrates this. From a population growth rate of about 2.5% in the early 1970s, Indonesia's rate of population growth declined to about 1.5% in the 1990s.

In South Asia, the rate of population growth also declined over time, but by not as much as in Southeast Asia. This is illustrated by the case of India, whose population growth rate declined from 2.5% in the 1960s to about 1.8% in the 1990s. However, in other South Asian countries, population growth rates in the 1990s (although lower than in the 1960s), still remain at relatively high levels. For the period 1980–2000, Pakistan's rate of population growth was still 2.6% per annum.

In the former Indo-Chinese states, population growth rates have also shown a downward trend, but with important variations. In the case of Vietnam, population growth rates fell significantly from the mid-1970s to the early 1980s, as the Communist victory in the Vietnam War led to large scale outward migration of "boat people". By the mid-1980s, the exodus of "boat people" had been brought under control, and Vietnam's population growth rose to reach 2.5% per annum. From then on, it continued to fall.

The general pattern, therefore, is one of declining population growth rates in most countries in Asia, with the most significant declines in East Asia and the least in South Asia.

The main reason for this declining trend in population growth rates was a significant fall in crude birth rates (with crude death rates remaining virtually unchanged). This is illustrated in Figure 6.2 using China as an example.

FIGURE 6.2: CRUDE BIRTH RATES AND
CRUDE DEATH RATES IN CHINA

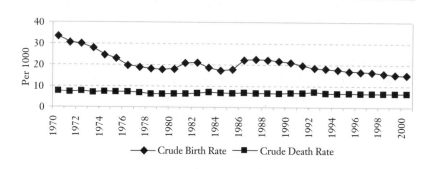

Source: State Statistical Bureau, *China Statistical Yearbook 2001*

As Figure 6.2 shows, China's crude birth rate fell steadily from the 1960s to the 1980s as family planning programmes and (later) the one-child policy was implemented. In the early 1980s, the crude birth rate started to rise unexpectedly. This turned out to be due to the "population momentum" effects (Tan 1999: 33–34) of the large increase in birth rates after the great famine in the early 1960s (when the crude birth rate increased to nearly 37 per thousand). In the early 1980s, many of the increased number of people who were born in the early 1960s (after the famine) had reached child-bearing age. This led to the rise in the crude birth rate in the early 1980s (Moran 1988: 79–80). In the mid-1980s, the crude birth rate increased again, this time, largely due to the market-oriented economic reforms (especially in agriculture) that encouraged larger family sizes. However, since the mid-1980s, China's crude birth rate has been falling. Note that from the 1970s, the crude death rate remained virtually unchanged (at about 6 per thousand). Thus, in China (as in many other Asian countries), the downward trend in population growth rates has been caused by reductions in the crude birth rate.

Another aspect of the slowing down on population growth in many Asian countries has been the decline in total fertility. This refers to the average number of children a woman will have, if her pattern of child-bearing is the same as an average woman in her age-group at different stages in her life. Thus the total fertility rate might be loosely interpreted as the average number a woman will have in her life-time. In Bangladesh, for example, the total fertility rate in 1978 was 6.1. By 1997 it had fallen to 3.2. This implies that average family sizes have been falling over time. This has contributed to the declining trend in population growth rates in many Asian countries.

FAMILY PLANNING PROGRAMMES

Although population growth rates normally decline as a country develops, many countries in the region have implemented family planning programmes designed to facilitate, or accelerate this process.

As a country develops, average incomes and living standards normally rise. The provision of health care improves as does access to education. Infant mortality usually falls, making it less necessary for couples to have a large number of children for fear that some of them will not survive to adulthood. Rising incomes also mean that there is less need for couples to have many children who are then sent to work in order to supplement family incomes. In addition, rising educational attainments enable people to become more aware of better pre-natal care, and better able to understand and practice family planning. In particular, as more women become educated, their employment opportunities increase, the age of marriage is often delayed, and the opportunity cost of time increases. These factors often lead to a decline in fertility as economic development progresses.

In many less developed countries, the factors which tend to cause a decline in the rate of population growth through the normal processes of economic development may be too slow because governments are already under much pressure to provide the resources needed to cater for a rapidly rising population. Family planning programmes are therefore implemented in order to accelerate the decline in population growth rates. Many countries in Asia implemented such programmes in the late 1960s when they became signatories to the United Nations Declaration on Population.

In many cases, the mere provision of the means of preventing unwanted births was not sufficient to persuade women to practice family planning, even when the costs of contraception were heavily subsidised or made freely available. Supplying the means of limiting family size was often not effective unless the factors which encouraged the demand for large families were neutralised. If infant mortality remained high, if there was a strong cultural preference for male children, or if there was strong religious opposition to family planning, contraception was unlikely to be practiced widely even if the means of preventing unwanted births were subsidised or provided at no cost. This explains some of the early failures of family planning programmes in countries such as India and China.

COERCIVE AND NON-COERCIVE POPULATION POLICIES

In some countries in Southeast and East Asia, coercive population policies were implemented in an attempt to reduce fertility significantly and quickly. The best example of this is the one-child policy in China.

China had begun to introduce family planning in the early 1970s with a programme of "planned births". Under this programme, the age of marriage was increased, the spacing of births was encouraged, and urban couples were urged to have only two children (three in rural areas). By the late 1970s, the crude birth rate had fallen to about 17 per thousand (it was over 30 per thousand in the 1960s), and the total fertility rate had declined to 2.6 (from 6.5 in the 1960s). In spite of this, China's population (which was 910 million in 1980) was still increasing by 19 million people each year. In 1979, a one-child policy was introduced. Under this policy, couples who had only one child, were given a welfare subsidy of three days' wages per month, an adult's grain ration until the child reached 14 years of age, one and a half shares of a private plot of land, and priority in medical treatment, education and employment. If the mother underwent sterilisation after the birth of the child, between 14 to 70 days of leave (depending on individual circumstances) with full pay would be granted.

If a couple had a second child, a number of financial penalties were imposed. This included giving up the land granted to the first child, a child-raising fee charged from the beginning of pregnancy until the second child reached the age of 14 years, and the sterilisation of the mother after the birth of the second child (and fines imposed if this was not done).

As a result of these coercive measures, the number of abortions in China increased to 14 million a year in 1983, and the number of sterilisation rose to 16 million. The rate of population growth stabilised at 1.3% per annum.

In spite of these strict measures, the one-child policy was widely circumvented, especially in rural areas where births were often not recorded and the infanticide of female children was widely practiced (Johanssen and Nygren 1991: 35–52). The one-child policy has also resulted in a number of unintended, but serious, consequences. China now has a whole generation of spoilt brats (Baker 1987: 43–44), many of whom will have much difficulty finding wives (since there are now many more males than females in young adulthood as a result of female infanticide). Every year, some 80,000 young women in China are abducted by desperate young men who are unable to find wives in the normal way (FEER 1997: 27).

Not all countries in Asia have implemented coercive family planning programmes. In countries such as Thailand and Indonesia, non-coercive family planning programmes have been very successful. In Indonesia, for example, the family planning programme has been implemented with widespread support at the grass-roots level. Religious leaders, community leaders, and village elders have been persuaded to support the programme. All the adults in the village are gathered together and the benefits of family planning are explained to them. Religious, community and village leaders then address the villagers, encouraging them to join the programme. Financial and other rewards are given to those who have participated in the family planning programme for a number of years (for example, educational scholarships for children), and communities which have a large number of participants in the programme are often rewarded with a new mosque, or a new paved road. The Indonesian family planning programme has been so successful that by the 1990s, its rate of population growth had declined to just below 2% per annum (from about 2.5% in the 1970s), and its total fertility rate had fallen to 3.3 (from 5.6 in the 1970s).

In a number of Asian countries, family planning programmes have not been implemented effectively (for religious and other reasons), and as a result, fertility decline in these countries has been slower than in other countries in the region. This is reflected in Table 6.1 which shows the total fertility rate and the contraceptive prevalence rate (percentage of women in Asian countries using contraceptives). The table shows that in South Asia, many countries (Sri Lanka is an exception) have relatively high total fertility rates and relatively low contraceptive prevalence rates. Pakistan stands out in this regard. A similar situation can be observed in the former Indo-Chinese states (where Myanmar and Vietnam are exceptions). Amongst ASEAN countries, Thailand and Indonesia have the lowest fertility rates, whilst fertility rates in the Asian NICs and in China are the lowest, and contraceptive prevalence rates are amongst the highest in the region.

In many parts of South Asia and in the Philippines, abject poverty and religious opposition have contributed to the absence of effective family planning programmes. In Cambodia and Laos, it is grinding poverty that has produced the same result. In the Asian NICs and China, rising levels of affluence plus coercive family planning policies in some countries have pushed total fertility rates to very low levels.

TABLE 6.1: TOTAL FERTILITY RATE AND CONTRACEPTIVE PREVALENCE RATE

Country	TFR	CPR
Bangladesh	3.1	54.0
India	3.1	57.0
Pakistan	4.7	28.0
Sri Lanka	2.1	62.0
Indonesia	2.5	57.0
Malaysia	3.0	48.0
Philippines	3.4	47.0
Thailand	1.9	72.0
Cambodia	4.0	NA
Laos	5.0	25.0
Myanmar	3.0	NA
Vietnam	2.2	75.0
Hong Kong SAR	1.0	83.0
Singapore	1.5	74.0
South Korea	1.4	79.0
Taiwan	NA	NA
China	1.9	83.0

Key: TFR = Total Fertility Rate in 2000

CPR = Contraceptive Prevalence Rate (% of women aged 15–49 years using contraceptives), 1990–2000.

Source: World Bank, *World Development Indicators 1997* and *2002*; Asian Development Bank 1997, *Emerging Asia: Changes and Challenges*, p. 148

FROM LABOUR SURPLUSES TO LABOUR SHORTAGES

During the 1950s and the 1960s, high population growth rates in many Asian countries led to labour surpluses as the number of people in the labour force increased significantly. This often led to high rates of unemployment in the 1960s.

Between 1960 and 1983, the proportion of the population of working age (15 to 64 years) increased from 54% to 56% in South Asia, from 53% to 57% in ASEAN countries, from 54% to 66% in the Asian NICs, and from 55% to 63% in China. In the 1960s, the

Asian NICs capitalised on the large increases in their labour forces
and embarked on labour-intensive export-oriented industrialisation.
China and the ASEAN countries followed suit in the late 1970s and
1980s respectively. The success of this strategy can be seen in the
case of Singapore. In 1957, only 67,000 persons in Singapore were
employed in the manufacturing sector. By 1994, this had swelled to
422,500 persons. In 1967, the unemployment rate in Singapore was
8.1%. By the late 1980s, Singapore had reached full employment. In
1990, its rate of unemployment was 1.7%. Indeed, by this time,
Singapore (like many other Asian NICs) was beginning to experience
acute labour shortages in a number of occupations.

Labour shortages

Between the 1960s and the 1980s, rapid economic growth, driven
by labour-intensive manufactured exports, led to labour shortages
in many of the Asian NICs. Declining fertility over a long period
of time did not help matters. With rising incomes and increasing
educational attainments, many people in the Asian NICs no longer
wanted to work in lower-paid occupations where conditions of work
were also poor (for example, as house maids or construction
workers). In addition, with industrialisation moving up the
technological ladder over time, the demand for various types of
skilled workers (especially engineers, scientists, and computer
programmers) outstripped the supply, leading to acute shortages
of labour (Tan 1995: 198–200).

In Singapore, the shortage of labour has affected one important
icon of the economy — Singapore Airlines. By the 1990s, even the
"Singapore Girl" (made famous in Singapore Airline advertisements
throughout the world) was increasingly not a Singaporean. Young
women in Singapore, increasingly well educated, were less and less
interested in becoming airline flight attendants especially as there
were other better paying jobs to which they could go. As a result,
Singapore Airlines had to recruit young women from neighbouring
countries (especially Malaysia, Thailand and China) to become
"Singapore Girls" (Hiebert 1995: 79).

Even in the ASEAN countries, sustained rapid economic growth in the 1980s led to shortages of unskilled, as well as skilled, labour. In Malaysia, shortages of unskilled labour began appearing in the late 1980s (Vatikiotis 1992: 46–47). By the late 1980s, Thailand was facing severe shortages of skilled labour (especially engineers) (Handley 1988: 96–97).

Migrant labour

In other parts of Asia, surplus labour is still available as a result of higher rates of population growth and large population bases. Large numbers of these people have been migrating to the Asian NICs, Japan (as well as to other parts of the world, such as the Middle East) as temporary (or guest) workers. While much of this flow of workers is regulated by host governments (through the issue of work permits and temporary visas), a large proportion is illegal, but tolerated by the host countries because they fill an excess demand for workers.

In many Southeast and East Asian countries, thousands of Filipinos and Indonesian women work as housemaids or nurses. Many endure poor working conditions and harsh treatment from their employers. Physical abuse, sexual harrassment, rape, and even murder have been reported in increasing numbers. Many married Indonesian and Filipino women who go abroad to work as maids, often discover that the husbands they left behind have quickly acquired new wives. This, and the hardship involved in being separated from their children, are some of the heavy costs that they have to bear for the sake of economic survival.

Thousands of young men from Bangladesh, Pakistan, India, Thailand and the Philippines work in construction sites or public works (such as road building) (do Rosario and Fairclough 1992: 20–21). Some countries, like Singapore, scour the world for skilled workers, attracting the best talent from around the globe (Hiebert 1996a: 67). Many people from developed countries (especially the USA, UK and Australia) now work in Singapore in professional occupations. In any given year, about 700,000 foreigners are working in Singapore. Many tens of thousands of people (mainly from Indonesia) are working in Malaysia (often illegally). This situation is repeated across Southeast and East Asia, in Brunei Darussalam, Hong Kong SAR, South Korea, Taiwan and Japan.

AGEING IN ASIAN SOCIETIES

One of the consequences of fertility decline and longer life expectancy in many Asian countries is a rapid ageing of the population. As fewer children are born over time, and as people live longer, the percentage of the elderly and aged (65 years of age and above) rises significantly. The associated increase in the aged dependency ratio means that an ever-larger percentage of the population has to be supported by a shrinking labour force. The implications of this, for the provision of health care, accommodation, and the financial needs of the aged, are staggering.

Table 6.2 shows the percentage of total population aged 65 years and above in Asian countries.

As Table 6.2 shows, the countries which are most likely to face problems associated with a rapidly ageing population are the Asian NICs, China, and Sri Lanka. In Hong Kong SAR, Singapore, South Korea (and most likely, Taiwan as well), the proportion of the population aged 65 years and above will rise significantly, and will exceed 10% by 2015. These ratios will approach those of developed countries (in 2015, the proportion of Australia's population that will be aged 65 years and above will be 15%). In Sri Lanka and China, the proportion will be just below 10%. By the year 2025, the proportions in many of these countries will be double what there were in 1995. This will put considerable strains on these economies, many of which do not have the institutions or resources to cater for a rapidly ageing population (Asian Development Bank 1997: 178–183; Hateley and Tan 2003).

TABLE 6.2: PERCENTAGE OF TOTAL POPULATION
AGED 65 YEARS AND ABOVE

Country	2000	2015
Bangladesh	3.1	4.1
India	5.0	5.9
Pakistan	3.7	3.7
Sir Lanka	6.3	9.1
Indonesia	4.8	6.0
Malaysia	4.1	6.0
Thailand	5.2	7.4
Philippines	3.5	5.1
Cambodia	2.8	3.9
Laos	3.5	3.3
Myanmar	4.6	5.3
Vietnam	5.3	4.8
Hong Kong SAR	10.6	13.4
Singapore	7.2	11.3
South Korea	7.1	10.8
Taiwan	8.0	NA
China	6.9	8.8

Source: World Bank, *World Development Indicators 2002*

The case of China illustrates the problems that will face many countries in Southeast and East Asia in the next 30 years or so. By 2030, some 250 million people (larger than the entire population of many other countries) in China will reach the age of 65 years. The proportion of the aged will increase to 14% of the total population (compared to 6% in 1985). At the same time, the number of working-age persons per aged person will decline from about ten in 1985, to four in 2030. This means that, whereas in 1985, there were ten working people to support one aged person, by 2030, there would only be four working people to support one aged person. Even with China's inadequate pension scheme for urban workers, the costs of retirement and other benefits (such as disability payments) will rise to 48% of total wages in 2030. This problem is compounded by the fact that, in China, people retire relatively early (at 60 years for men, and 55 years

111

for women), compared to average life expectancy (which was 70 years in 1997). Unless China changes its pension scheme, the economy will not be able to bear the burdens of a rapidly ageing population in 2030 (Delfs 1990: 17–18).

The problem of ageing in many Southeast and East Asian countries is compounded by the gradual breakdown of the extended family system. With increasing modernisation and urbanisation, the trend has been towards nuclear families. As a result, aged parents can no longer be confident that their children will look after them in their old age. This, combined with inadequate pension schemes spell a grim future for the aged in many Asian countries.

In Singapore, new laws were passed in 1996 to enable parents to sue their children for neglecting to take care of them in their old age. A new court was established to hear cases in which parents can sue their children for maintenance. Within a month of its establishment, some 60 such cases were filed (Hiebert 1996b: 42).

CONCLUSION

Population growth rates have been falling in many countries in Asia since the 1950s. The most sustained, and most pronounced decline have taken place in the Asian NICs and in China. The least have been observed in South Asia (especially Bangladesh and Pakistan), and in some countries in Southeast Asia (such as the Philippines). The downward trend in rates of population growth in many parts of Asia has been due to the general increase in economic development, as well as the implementation of family programmes by governments keen on accelerating the process of fertility decline.

Some countries have used coercive family planning programmes to force population growth rates down. These often employ punitive financial disincentives to those who do not limit their family size, and generous financial incentives to those who do. Other countries have employed non-coercive family planning programmes with equal success. A combination of financial incentives and intensive education programmes have often been used.

The long-term decline in population growth rates has resulted in some countries (especially the Asian NICs, but also some ASEAN countries) experiencing labour shortages by the 1980s. These have been filled by migrant labour from the labour surplus countries in the region (such as the Philippines).

Another important consequence of declining fertility in many Asian countries has been a rapid ageing of the population. By the first few decades of the 21st century, many countries in the region will have much larger proportions of their populations in the ages of 65 years and above. In some countries (such as China), the number of those in this age group will be in the hundred of millions, larger than the total populations of many other countries. The strains that this will put on government services (such as health care) for the aged, and on inadequate pension schemes, will be enormous.

CHAPTER 7

Education

INTRODUCTION

Education has always played an important role in Asian societies. In countries where Confucian values have been dominant, reverence for learning and respect for teachers have been important influences on societal attitudes towards education. Education is regarded, not only as of intrinsic value, but also as a means of upward social mobility. Parents make great personal sacrifices in order to ensure that their children obtain the best education possible. In countries where other values prevailed, education is still regarded highly, and governments make great efforts to make education accessible to as many people as possible.

Since the end of the Second World War, when many countries in Asia attained political independence, there has been a tremendous expansion of all levels of education. This was partly to redress the lack of educational facilities that prevailed during colonial times. With rare exceptions, colonial governments were loath to provide education for the people over whom they ruled, for fear that this could awaken political consciousness, and stir demands for political independence. The post-war expansion of education in many Asian countries was also due to the realisation that an educated workforce was essential for subsequent economic growth and development.

EDUCATION AND DEVELOPMENT

Education has long been recognised as an important ingredient in the process of economic growth and development (McClelland 1966: 257–78). A highly educated workforce is

114

more likely to be more productive, more able to absorb and adapt new technology, more adept at operating and maintaining sophisticated machinery, more capable of exploring new ways of doing things, and more likely to be able to embark on research and development of new ideas.

In addition, certain types of foreign investment which employ capital and/or skill intensive technologies are often attracted to countries where a highly educated workforce is available, not only in the form of skilled production workers, but also in terms of able supervisors, engineers, scientists, administrators, and managers. Countries which start with industrial development based on the manufacture of products using unskilled labour, usually find that they are unable to move up the "technological ladder" into the manufacture of more sophisticated products because they lack the necessary skills in their workers (Crispin 1999: 45).

The more developed a country is, the higher the educational attainments in its population are likely to be. For reasons outlined above, education is likely to be positively associated with economic development. This is shown in Figure 7.1 which shows secondary school enrolments of selected countries at different levels of economic development (using per capita GDP as an indicator). As Figure 7.1 shows, there is a broad positive relationship between education (as measured by the percentage of the relevant age group enrolled in secondary schools), and the level of economic development (using per capita GNP as a percentage of Singapore's per capita GNP). The higher the level of economic development, the higher the secondary enrolment rate. Singapore and Hong Kong SAR (not shown in Figure 7.1) have higher average incomes than South Korea and Taiwan, but lower secondary school enrolment rates. The reason for this is that South Korea and Taiwan inherited the Japanese (and later American) system of education, whilst Singapore and Hong Kong SAR inherited the more elitist British education system.

FIGURE 7.1: EDUCATION AND ECONOMIC
DEVELOPMENT, 2000

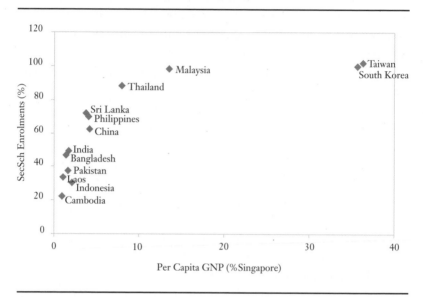

Sources: World Bank, *World Development Indicators 2002*; Council of Economic
Planning and Development, *Taiwan Statistical Data Book 2002*

Part of the reason for the positive relationship between
education and development shown in Figure 7.1 is that more
developed countries are better able to afford the costs of, and
provide the resources for, the education to their populations.
There is, however, also a causal relationship between education
and development. As explained above, a better educated workforce
is likely to enhance and accelerate economic growth and
development.

One way of demonstrating this causal relationship is to test
its implications. Countries with high educational attainment in a
given year are more likely to achieve higher rates of economic
growth in future years. This is illustrated in Figure 7.2, which
plots primary school enrolment rates in 1980 against GDP growth
rates for the period 1980–90. If education has a causal effect on
economic growth, we would expect to see a positive relationship

116

between primary school enrolment rates in 1980, and rates of economic growth in the subsequent period, 1980–90. High enrolment rates in primary schools in 1980 are likely to have flowed through to high enrolment rates in secondary and tertiary levels of education, leading to high average levels of schooling in the labour force.

Figure 7.2 shows some confirmation of this. There is a broad positive relationship between the two variables. Countries, such as Bangladesh or India, which had very low primary school enrolment rates in 1980, also had low rates of economic growth in 1980–90. At the other end of the spectrum, countries such as South Korea and Taiwan which had very high enrolment rates in primary schools in 1980, also had very high growth rates in 1980–90. By the 1990s, the average years of schooling in the labour force in countries like South Korea and Taiwan was about seven years, while for India and Bangladesh, it was about three years. Thus the data do provide some support for the view that education plays a very important (and causal) role in economic growth and development. If a negative relationship had been observed between primary school enrolment rates in 1980, and economic growth in 1980–90, the view that education plays a causal, positive role in economic growth and development, would have been difficult to sustain. Sri Lanka and the Philippines (not shown in Figure 7.2) are exceptions. In these countries, high primary enrolment ratios have been accompanied by low economic growth. In Sri Lanka, this has been due to a long period of internal warfare, whilst in the Philippines, chronic economic mismanagement has resulted in that country being dubbed "the poor man of Asia".

**FIGURE 7.2: EDUCATION AND ECONOMIC GROWTH,
1980 AND 1980–90**

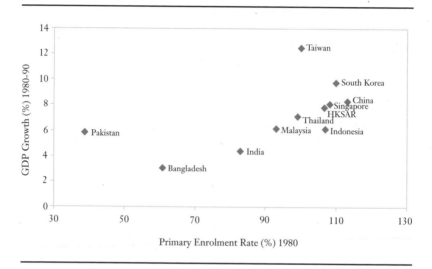

Souce: World Bank, *World Development Report* (various issues)

THE EXPANSION OF EDUCATION

The post-Second World War period saw a rapid expansion of education in many Asian countries. Governments of these countries (many of them newly independent), invested heavily in education. The number of students in all levels of education increased substantially As a result of this, most countries reached universal primary education by the 1980s. This is reflected in high literacy rates by the 1990s. In many countries, the expansion of secondary and tertiary education also resulted in high enrolments rates and large numbers of students in these levels of education by the 1990s.

The case of Taiwan illustrates these trends. Figure 7.3 shows Taiwanese government expenditure on education as a percentage of GDP and total government expenditures. The figure shows that for most of the period between 1952 and 1997, educational expenditures were a rising share of both GDP and total government expenditures. In 1952, government expenditure on education was NT$892 million.

By 1997, it had grown to NT$397,128 million. During the period 1952–97, educational expenditure as a percentage of GDP rose from 3% to about 6%. During the same period, educational expenditure as a percentage of total government expenditure rose from 14% to about 20%. This is a reflection of the importance that the Taiwanese government placed on education. Many other governments in Asia took a similar view.

FIGURE 7.3: TAIWAN — GOVERNMENT EXPENDITURE ON EDUCATION

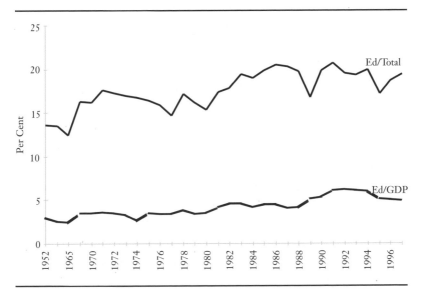

Source: Council for Economic Planning and Development, *Taiwan Statistical Data Book 1998*

In Taiwan, the number of students receiving education (at all levels) increased from 1.18 million in 1952 to 5.2 million in 1997. Most of this increase was concentrated in secondary and tertiary levels. With declining population growth rates during the period concerned, enrolments in primary schools increased by an average of only 0.06% per annum. From the early 1970s onwards, enrolments in primary schools declined steadily. In secondary schools, enrolments increased by an average of 4% per annum during 1952–97, with positive growth in most years. By the mid-1990s, enrolments in secondary schools had also started to decline (as a result of declining fertility over time). It is in tertiary education that enrolments have increased at an impressive rate (averaging 7.4% growth per annum, and accelerating in the 1980s and 1990s).

Thus, in Taiwan, as in many other Asian countries, the expansion of education has been a significant feature of economic development in the post-war period.

EDUCATIONAL ATTAINMENTS

As a result of large and sustained investments in education over many years, many Southeast and East Asian countries recorded high educational attainments by the 1990s. Enrolments in primary school were universal in many countries, while secondary school enrolment rates approached those of many developed countries. Enrolment rates in tertiary education varied, but even at this level, they were comparable with many developed countries. Another important aspect of educational attainments is that in many Asian NICs, large numbers of scientists and engineers were trained. Table 7.1 displays the relevant data. The table shows that, by 2000, most countries had achieved universal primary education (enrolment ratios of greater than 100% indicate the presence of overaged students). Secondary enrolment ratios vary considerably between countries. The lowest enrolment rates in secondary education are found in the former Indo-Chinese countries, while the highest are found in the Asian NICs. In Southeast Asia, most countries have high secondary enrolment ratios. The exception is Indonesia, whose secondary enrolment ratio is similar to that of India and Bangladesh.

TABLE 7.1: EDUCATION ENROLMENT RATIOS, 2000

Country	Primary	Secondary	Tertiary
India	100	49	7
Bangladesh	122	49	5
Pakistan	86	37	3
Sri Lanka	111	71	5
Indonesia	115	48	11
Malaysia	99	98	11
Philippines	116	77	28
Thailand	94	88	30
Cambodia	119	22	1
Laos	111	33	3
Myanmar	114	36	6
Vietnam	110	61	11
Hong Kong SAR	107	73	28
Singapore	192	67	39
South Korea	94	102	60
Taiwan	117	100	55
China	107	62	6

Source: World Bank, *World Development Indicators 2002*; Council for Economic Planning and Development, *Taiwan Statistical Data Book 2002*

In tertiary education, the highest enrolment rates are found in the Asian NICs, especially in South Korea and Taiwan (which adopted the American system of higher education). High enrolment rates are also found in the Philippines and Thailand (which also adopted the American system of higher education). The lowest enrolment rates in tertiary education are found in the former Indo-Chinese states, in South Asia, and in China.

One important feature of the educational development of many Asian countries is the high proportion of scientists and engineers that are trained each year. In Singapore, some 57% of university undergraduates are studying science and engineering, while in Hong Kong SAR, the ratio is 43%. In the Philippines, some 38% of university students study science and engineering, while in South Korea and Taiwan, the ratio is around 30%. This compares favourably with some developed countries such as Australia where approximately 24% of university students study science and engineering. In 2002, a survey was published by UNICEF that showed that of all the developed countries, South Korea scored the highest in terms of the ability of 14- and 15-year-olds at reading, mathematics and science (The Straits Times 2002a: A1).

THE QUALITY OF EDUCATION

The quality of education varies considerably between Asian countries. Some countries which inherited the British or Japanese system of education, and which have continued to invest in education and to raise standards, have a high quality of education. The Asian NICs fall into this category.

The high quality of education in the Asian NICs is reflected in their performance in international mathematics and science competitions. In 1995, Singapore ranked first, South Korea ranked third, and Hong Kong SAR ranked fifth in international competitions in science and mathematics amongst secondary school students.

An example of the high quality of education in some countries in Asia can be seen in the Cambridge University O-Level results of the Singapore Chinese Girls' School in 1997. Of 211 girls who sat this examination, 94.3% obtained passes in seven subjects, 99.5% obtained passes in five subjects, while 100% obtained passes in three subjects. Furthermore, in English, the pass rate was 100%, and of these 72% received distinctions. In Mathematics D, 100% passed and 94% received distinctions. In Chemistry and Geography, 100% passed and 80% received distinctions (Scanner 1998:1).

In 1997, a survey of the best 50 universities in Asia placed the University of Hong Kong at 3rd, the National University of Singapore at 4th, the Chinese University of Hong Kong at 5th (ahead of the University of New South Wales, Australia), National Taiwan University at 8th (ahead of the University of Melbourne), Hong Kong University of Science and Technology at 10th (ahead of the Australian National University and the University of Sydney), Nanyang Technological University (Singapore) at 15th,

Seoul National University at 16th (both ahead of Monash University, Australia), and Yonsei University (South Korea) at 18th (ahead of the University of Queensland, Australia).

In countries which inherited other systems of education (especially those which encouraged private schools and universities), and/or did not continue to invest in education or upgrade standards, the quality of education is very uneven. Often, a very small number of high quality educational institutions is surrounded by a sea of mediocre establishments. The Philippines provides a good example of this. The rapid expansion of education during the post-Second World War period has resulted in a large number of institutions, many of which are privately funded, and are of dubious quality. This has resulted in a steady decline in the quality of education in the Philippines (Tiglao and Scottt 1989:38).

In tertiary education, many countries in the region abandoned the "international audit", discouraging the employment of foreign academics from reputable universities. Many of their staff do not often publish in international refereed journals, or with reputable publishing houses.

In 1992, the University of Allahabad's (a well-known Indian University) department of Physics had 29 academic staff, all of whom (ranging from professors to lecturers) took all their degrees from the University of Allahabad (Commonwealth Universities Yearbook 1992: 1657). This is often the case in many other Indian universities. By contrast, the University of Singapore's department of Physics had 36 academic staff in 1992. All had degrees from some of the most reputable universities in the world (for example, six had degrees from Oxbridge, four from London, four from other UK universities, ten had degrees from good US universities, three had degrees from reputable Canadian universities, and two had degrees from good universities in Australia and New Zealand). In addition, apart from Singaporeans and Malaysians, the staff of the University of Singapore's Physics department included academics from seven other countries (Hong Kong SAR, Taiwan, India, USA, UK, China, and Croatia) (Commonwealth Universities Yearbook 1992: 2695).

In spite of the high level of academic excellence in many Asian countries, the quality of education is marred by an overemphasis on rote-learning, rather than independent, critical and innovative thinking. In a survey carried out by the prestigious University of Tokyo in 2003, companies that hired a large number of graduates from the university gave such employees top marks for their ability to work hard on their own. They were less successful when it came to creative output or risk-taking. A poll taken by *Asahi Shimbun* amongst senior executives of Japan's leading 100 firms revealed that logical thinking, creativity and problem-solving were amongst the top three attributes that Japanese university graduates lacked (Kwan 2003: A3).

The high regard that many people in the region place on learning and on teachers has often led to an unquestioning acceptance of what is taught. While this may not have been a problem in the early phases of industrial development, it is a serious handicap in later phases, in which the creation of new processes and new products is vital. For this reason, some countries in the region have taken steps toward the difficult task of encouraging creativity (Hiebert 1996c: 29–30; Dolven 1998: 47–49).

EDUCATION AND FERTILITY

One of the most important aspects of the development of many countries in Southeast and East Asia, has been the relationship between education and fertility. As educational attainments rise (especially amongst women), fertility rates usually fall. Several factors account for this. The more educated women are, the more likely are they to obtain employment outside the home. This tends to delay the age of marriage (Anderson, Hill and Butler 1987: 223–234), and therefore shorten the time span of reproductive years. More educated women are also more likely to be aware of, understand, and to adopt contraception and family planning. Some economists also believe that education increases the opportunity costs of womens' time, making educated women less likely to want large families (Tan 1999:39–45).

The rising age of marriage also tends to lower fertility. As people become more educated and seek to further their careers, the age of marriage usually rises. The older a woman is when she marries, the higher is the probability that she will be infertile. A study in the USA indicated that between 30% and 50% of highly educated, high-achieving career women in that country were childless, and most were childless not by choice (Long 2002: 29).

In many Asian countries, increasing proportions of highly educated women remain unmarried. In some cases, this is an act of free choice with many educated women preferring to remain single (Daorueng 1998: 36–37). In other cases, highly educated women have remained single because of the difficulty of finding suitable marriage partners. Often, highly educated women avoid marrying men who are less educated than they are, while highly educated men tend to avoid marrying women who are more highly educated than they are. In 1990, 76% of women university graduates in Singapore married men who were also university graduates. On the other hand, 63% of male university graduates married women with lower educational qualifications than themselves (Singapore Census of Population 1990: 13).

As a result of this, the proportion of educated Singapore women (those with university degrees) who are unmarried has risen steadily over the years (Balakrishnan 1991: 17). In 1980, 14% of women university graduates aged 20–24 years remained unmarried. By 2000, this had risen to 49%. Over the same interval of time, the proportion of women university graduates aged 25–29 years increased from 15% to 72% (Singapore Census of Population 1990: 14, 2000: 72–78). A survey in Singapore showed that while 80% of women in their 20s thought that marrying was better than staying single, only 48% of women in their 30s thought so. In addition, 88% of women in their 20s thought that married couples should have children, while only 50% of women in their 30s shared this view (Wong and Sim 2002: H1). These trends have caused so much anxiety amongst policy makers that the government has established a Social Development Unit in order to bring unmarried graduates together (in parties and cruises) in the hope that nature will then take its course (Balakrishnan 1989a: 38). Its success rate has not been spectacular.

Figure 7.4 plots the difference between the female and male adult illiteracy rate against the fertility rate in countries for which data are available.

FIGURE 7.4: FEMALE EDUCATION AND FERTILITY, 2000

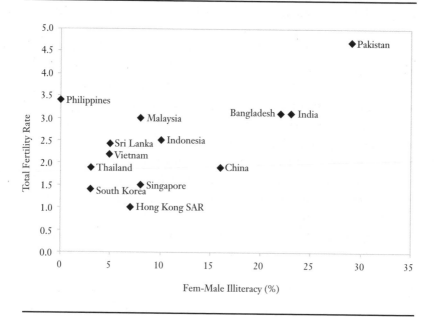

Source: World Bank, *World Development Indicators 2002*

Figure 7.4 shows that there is a broad positive relationship between the difference in the female to male adult illiteracy rate and the fertility rate. Countries like Pakistan and Bangladesh, where the adult female illiteracy rate is much higher than the adult male illiteracy rate, have much higher fertility rates than countries like South Korea and Hong Kong SAR, where the difference between adult female and male illiteracy rates is small. The Philippines is an outlier. There, extreme poverty and religious opposition to contraception have resulted in a relatively high fertility rate, given its very small difference between adult female to male illiteracy rates.

It is no accident that countries (like Singapore and Hong Kong SAR) have some of the lowest fertility rates, and some of the highest standards of living. Declining fertility rates have allowed these countries to allocate their scarce resources in productive investment, and to increase the quantity and quality of government services per head of population.

CONCLUSION

One of the most significant developments in Asia since the Second World War has been the rapid expansion of education. Many countries in Asia now have universal primary education, and several have enrolments rates in secondary and tertiary education which approach those of developed countries. Many countries have invested heavily in education. This has helped to underpin rapid economic growth in these countries.

One important feature of educational development in Asian countries has been the increasing importance in the training of scientists and engineers, especially in the Asian NICs. This has allowed them to move up the technological ladder, into the manufacture of more capital and skill-intensive manufactured exports.

Another important feature of educational development in Asian countries has been in increasing access of education to women. Most countries have closed the gender gaps in primary and secondary education, although in tertiary education, there is still some way to go.

While the quality of education varies between Asian countries, some (such as the Asian NICs) have some of the highest standards of education in the region, if not in the world. However, most countries suffer from an overemphasis on rote learning at the expense of independent, critical thinking.

Increasing education attainments in many Asian countries have enabled them to increase the productivity of their labour force and to attract foreign investment, thus boosting industrial growth and economic development. Rising educational attainments (especially of women) have also resulted in declining fertility in many countries. This has helped to increase standards of living.

CHAPTER **8**

The Role of Women

INTRODUCTION

Women play a very important role in any society, not only as individuals, companions, wives and mothers, but also as workers in many fields of endeavour. Although they make up approximately half of society, and perform most of the work that needs to be done, they are frequently inadequately paid and often unappreciated. Nowhere is this more evident than in many Asian countries where the status and well-being of women are often given low priority.

Few countries in the region devote resources, or provide opportunities to women that is in anyway commensurate with their contribution to society. In terms of education, employment, health, and other services, women tend to be disproportionately disadvantaged in many Asian countries. This is not peculiar to Asia. It is true of all countries in the world even the most developed ones (United Nations Development Programme 1995: 2–3). In many Asian countries, however, the unequal treatment of women is more acute.

THE EDUCATION OF WOMEN

In many Asian countries, females are not given education to the same extent as males. It is often considered by parents to be a waste of money to educate daughters since they will eventually marry and leave home. Before they marry, daughters stay at home to help their mothers with household chores (or work in the fields) and to look after younger siblings. After they marry, they are unlikely to work so spending money on educating daughters is often thought to be a waste of scarce resources. On the other hand, sons are more likely to work, remain with their parents (even after they marry), and look after them in their old age. The education of sons, is therefore considered more important than the education of daughters.

In most Asian countries for which data are available in the late 1990s, the gender gap in primary education has been closed. Countries with the lowest ratios of females to total students in primary school were Laos (43%), India (43%), and Cambodia (45%). Female illiteracy rates are relatively low for several Asian countries. In Vietnam and Thailand, only about 16% and 10% respectively, of adult females were illiterate in the late 1990s, while in the Philippines, the proportion was also 10%. However, in Bangladesh, Cambodia, China and Pakistan, more than 75% of adult females were illiterate. In India, the proportion was 66%. For many other Asian countries (such as Laos, Malaysia, and Myanmar), about 25% of adult females were illiterate) (Economic Commission for Asia and the Pacific 1998: 185).

Data of enrolment at secondary school level according to gender are not available for many Asian countries, but for those for which data are available, many countries (such as the Asian NICs, the Philippines and Sri Lanka) have closed the gender gap. In some countries (such as Sri Lanka), female enrolment rates in secondary schools are equal or higher than that of males. However, in Laos, females made up only 39% of total enrolments in secondary school, while in Indonesia it was 45%.

At the tertiary level, gender gaps varied considerably between Asian countries. In Cambodia, only 16% of those enrolled in tertiary education were females, while in Vietnam, the proportion was 24%. On the other hand, in Myanmar, 61% of those enrolled in tertiary education were females, while in the Philippines, the ratio was 57%. In many other countries (including the Asian NICs), the proportion was between 35% and 44%.

Thus, in terms of gender gaps in education, the most significant advances have been made in primary education where in most Asian countries, the gender gap has been closed. In Bangladesh, India, Pakistan and Laos, female enrolment rates in primary schools in the early 1990s were still between 55% (Pakistan) and 86% (Bangladesh and Laos) of male enrolment rates, but even in these countries, these rates are significantly higher than what they were in the 1970s.

This is largely true of the gender gap in secondary education, although the lack of data for many countries makes it difficult to confirm this. By the early 1990s, the gender gap in secondary school enrolments had been closed (or nearly closed) in the Asian NICs and in some ASEAN countries (such as Malaysia, the Philippines, Indonesia and Vietnam). However, in South Asia, and in some of the former Indo-Chinese states, female enrolment rates in secondary schools ranged from 44% (Pakistan) to 60% (India and Laos). These rates were, nevertheless, significant improvements over what they were in the 1970s.

In tertiary education, however, the gender gap is still significant, even in the Asian NICs, which are amongst the most developed Asian countries. In South Korea, female enrolment rates in tertiary education in 1990 was only 53% of male enrolment rates, while for Hong Kong SAR and Singapore, the rates were 71% and 85% respectively. In Bangladesh and Pakistan, female enrolment rates in tertiary education were between 27% and 38% of male enrolment rates, while in India, the ratio was 50%.. There are some notable exceptions to the gender gap in tertiary education in Asian countries. In Malaysia, the Philippines, Sri Lanka, Myanmar, and Vietnam, the female enrolment rates in tertiary education was equal to or greater than the enrolment rates of males. In most countries, there has been a significant improvement in the enrolment rates of females in tertiary education, compared to male enrolment rates.

In many Asian countries, the mean years of schooling of adult females (aged 25 years or more) is high compared to that of males. In 1994, the mean years of schooling of adult females in Malaysia was 5 years (compared to 5.6 years for adult males). In the Philippines, it was 7 years (compared to 7.8 years for adult males), while in Sri Lanka, it was 6.1 years (compared to 7.7 years for adult males). However, there are some countries where there was a large difference between the mean years of schooling between adult females and males. In Bangladesh, India and Pakistan, the mean years of schooling for adult females was one year (compared to three years for adult males). In other countries (such as China, Indonesia, Thailand and Vietnam), the mean years of schooling of adult females was about three years (compared to between four to six years for adult males) (Economic Commission for Asia and the Pacific 1998: 185).

THE EMPLOYMENT OF WOMEN

Female labour force participation rate

Increasing educational opportunities for women usually translate into widening employment opportunities. Countries which have high female enrolment rates in education would normally also have high rates of participation of women in the labour force. This is shown in Figure 8.1 in which the ratio of female to male labour force participation rates is plotted against the difference between female and male adult illiteracy rates. In countries (such as Pakistan and India) where the female adult illiteracy rate is much higher than that of males, the female labour force participation rate is much lower than that of males.

FIGURE 8.1: FEMALE LABOUR FORCE PARTICIPATION RATES AND FEMALE EDUCATION, 2000

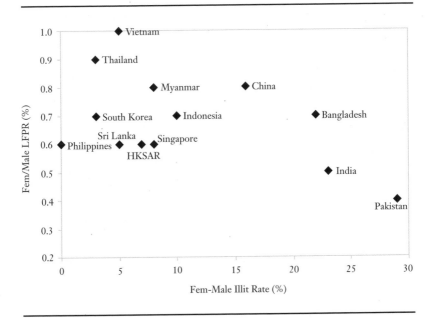

Source: World Bank, *World Development Indicators 2002*

On the other hand, in countries (such as Vietnam and Thailand) where the difference between the female and male adult literacy rates is small, the female labour force participation rate is not very different from that of males. A number of outliers should be noted. In the Philippines, the difference between female and male adult illiteracy rates is small. Yet the ratio of the female to male labour force participation rates is not as high as might be expected. The reason for this is that years of economic mis-management has resulted in the Philippines not being able to create sufficient jobs for its people. In South Korea, the difference between female and male adult illiteracy rates is also low, but the ratio of female to male labour force participation rates is not as high as might be expected. The reason for this is that in South Korea, cultural values and social attitudes regarding the role of women in society mean that, in spite of their high levels of education, relatively few South Korean women work (Rolton and Cason 1996: 12).

In spite of these outliers, Figure 8.1 shows that there is a broad inverse relationship between female education and female participation in the workforce. Increasing educational attainments of women usually result in a high proportion of women participating in the workforce. This is particularly evident in the Asian NICs (except South Korea), and the ASEAN countries (except the Philippines). By contrast, many countries in South Asia have relatively low female labour force participation rates as well as low levels of educational attainments of females.

In Singapore, the female participation rate in the labour force has been heightened, not only by rising educational attainments of women, but also because of labour shortages. Rapid economic growth and the fact that males have to spend two and a half years performing National Service, has caused labour shortages which have given women greater opportunities in employment (Balakrishnan 1989b: 34–35). In some age groups (for example, 20–24 years), the female participation rate in the labour force (73% in 1998) is higher than that of males (70%). In 1967, only 30% of those employed in Singapore were females. By 1997, this ratio had risen to approximately 40%.

Structure of employment of women

In many Asian countries, women tend to dominate the lower-paid occupations, such as agricultural workers, clerical services, domestic services, food-vending, etc. Within the occupations in which women are found, they are usually paid less than men in similar occupations. The concentration of women in lower-paid occupations and the lower wages they earn relative to men, is partly a reflection of their lower levels of educational attainments, skills and experience. It is also a reflection of discrimination in the labour market where women are often thought to be less able in certain kinds of jobs, or less reliable, in terms of the frequency of illness and absenteeism. Although these sentiments are present in developed countries, they are often more pronounced in less developed countries.

Table 8.1 shows the occupational distribution of women in several Asian countries for which data are available. The data pertains to 1990 as more recent data was not available.

TABLE 8.1: OCCUPATIONAL DISTRIBUTION OF WOMEN, 1990

Country	Admin	Prof	Clerk	Serv
Bangladesh	5.1	23.1	4.2	46.4
Pakistan	3.0	18.4	2.8	13.9
Sri Lanka	6.9	49.6	22.1	37.7
Brunei	11.3	35.3	52.2	40.2
Indonesia	6.6	40.8	44.2	57.5
Philippines	27.7	63.2	62.7	58.0
Thailand	22.2	52.7	57.3	56.1
Hong Kong SAR	11.6	45.1	39.3	51.7
Singapore	15.7	40.3	NA	40.8
South Korea	4.1	42.5	44.0	60.9
China	11.6	45.1	39.3	51.7

Key: Admin = **Administrative and Managerial occupations**
   Prof = **Professional, Technical, and related occupations**
   Clerk = **Clerical and Sales occupations**
   Serv = **Service occupations**
Source: United Nations Development Programme, *Human Development Report 1995*

As Table 8.1 shows, with the exception of the Philippines and Thailand, women account for small proportions of administrative and managerial staff in most countries. In professional, scientific and related occupations, women account for between 40% and 63% of those employed, except for Bangladesh, Brunei, and Pakistan, where the share of women is much smaller. In clerical and sales, there is a wide variation in the share of women in total employment, with some countries (for example, Bangladesh and Pakistan) registering very small shares and other countries (for example, the Philippines and Thailand), registering large shares. In service occupations, women account for between 40% and 60% of those employed in most countries except Pakistan and Sri Lanka, where lower shares are evident. On the whole, the table shows that women are least represented in the administrative and managerial occupations.

Some aspects of the role and status of women in 2002 can be found in the *Human Development Report 2003*. In that year, the percentage of women legislators, senior officials and managers, as a percentage of males in those positions, ranged from 4%–5% in Bangladesh, Sri Lanka and South Korea, to 23%–27% in Singapore, Hong Kong SAR and Thailand. Only in the Philippines was the ratio higher (35%). In terms of the percentage of females employed in Professional, Technical and Services, the ratio ranged from 26% in Pakistan, to 35%–49% in Bangladesh and Sri Lanka. Only in Thailand (55%) and the Philippines (66%) were the ratios higher (World Bank 2003: 226–228).

In terms of pay, women are usually paid less than men in most Asian countries. At one end of the scale, women in Bangladesh are paid only 43% of male wages, whilst at the other end, women in Vietnam are paid 91.5% of male wages. In the Asian NICs, the ratio is about 70% except for South Korea (where it is 53.5%). This situation was virtually unchanged in 2002 (World Bank 2003: 226–228). In ASEAN countries (such as Thailand and the Philippines), the ratio is between 60% and 70%. In most countries, women work longer hours than men. In the rural areas of many countries (for example, the Philippines), women work 20% longer than men (United National Development Programme 1995: 91).

With the rapid industrialisation of many Southeast and East Asian countries since the 1960s, large numbers of women have been employed in labour-intensive export industries such as electronics component assembly, clothing, footwear, and toys. In Malaysia, for example, large numbers (more than 120,000 in the late 1980s) of young Malay women have moved to the Export Processing Zones (especially on the island of Penang) to work in electronics factories. Although this has brought some benefits to them in terms of higher incomes, better standards of living, and greater independence (compared to their situations previously), it has also resulted in psychological and social problems which flow from a sudden change in lifestyle and social environment. Conditions of work are often poor, wages low, and mistreatment ranging from abusive behaviour to sexual harassment by male supervisors are commonplace (Scott 1989: 32–34). Women in other Asian countries have had similar experiences (Tipton 1998: 393–403).

Unpaid work of women

Much of the work of women, in the home or in the fields, is unpaid and unrecorded. In most countries (including developed ones), some 66% of womens' time is spent in unpaid work. In some Asian countries (for example, the Philippines), the ratio is above 70%. While estimates for less developed countries are not available, studies for developed countries suggest that the value of the unpaid work of women in developed countries is very large, amounting to at least 50% of GDP (United Nations Development Programme 1995: 89–97).

WOMEN IN ASIAN SOCIETIES

The well-being of women in Asian societies is reflected in a number of indicators which affect them directly, and which reflect the extent to which resources are devoted to their well-being, or the degree to which economic and other pressures are brought to bear on them.

In rural China, women often have to bear the crushing burden of agricultural work and the responsibilities of looking after their children on their own as their husbands go to towns and cities in search of work (frequently, they also find female partners as well). This is one of the factors which has resulted in an alarmingly high rate of female suicide in China. China contains 21% of the world's women, but accounts for 56% of the world's female suicides. Other factors include unhappy, arranged marriages, and the strict implementation of China's one-child policy (which used to result in the home of a woman who has had, or is expecting, her second child, demolished) (MacLeod 1998: 62–63).

In Pakistan, women have been murdered just for asking for a divorce from their abusive husbands. Often, their families collude in their murders, as a dead daughter is preferable to a divorced one (men can divorce and re-marry as many times as they wish, and are allowed to have up to four wives at any one time). In some parts of Pakistan, many women are killed each year as a result of the practice of *karo kiri*, in which people involved in (or accused of) illicit sexual relationships are killed in order to preserve the honour of their families (these killings are known as "honour killings"). Often the killers are let off without punishment, or are punished only lightly, as *karo kiri* killings are considered as crimes passionnels. Such killings are not restricted to the rural or uneducated. They transcend class, religion, education and ethnicity (Islam 1999:28–29). In a recent case, a young Pakistani woman who had been repeatedly raped, applied to the court for redress. She was sent back to her village, where her case was to be considered by the village elders. There, she was reportedly shot for bringing dishonour to her family.

For centuries, Japanese women have been treated as second-class citizens. Their role in society was to serve men as wives, mistresses and mothers (a role epitomised in airline advertisements featuring beautiful flight attendants, tucking male passengers to sleep in long-haul flights). Japanese women are trained from a young age to speak in an unnatural high-pitched (almost *sotto voce*) voice, and to behave in a deferrential, and submissive, manner towards men.

In the workplace, Japanese women are often discriminated against in terms of pay and conditions of work (often they are forced to leave if they fall pregnant), and have to put up with sexual harassment from their male co-workers or bosses. Despite the fact that Japanese women are some of the most highly educated in the world, once they marry, they are expected to stop working and to become full-time wives and mothers (do Rosario 1992: 40–41). Nowhere is this more poignantly illustrated than in the case of Empress Masako, a Harvard-educated former diplomat, who receded into the background after she married the then Crown Prince Akihito. In April 1999, a new and more effective equal opportunity law and a gender equality law came into effect in Japan. These promise to give Japanese women legal protection in their quest to achieve equal rights with men (Amaha 1999: 34–36).

South Korean women have, for years, suffered the same indignities as their Japanese counterparts. Sexual harassment in the workplace, and the allocation of certain tasks to women (such as the making of drinks for men), have been commonplace in South Korea. In January 1999, the South Korean National Assembly passed a revised equal opportunity law making it compulsory for all firms employing more than ten people to provide annual training programmes designed to stamp out sexual harassment in the workplace (Song 1999: 35).

Every year, tens of thousands of migrant workers leave the poorer countries of Asia (such as Bangladesh or India) to work in the richer countries of Asia (such as Singapore or Hong Kong SAR). Many go further afield to developed countries such as the USA and Canada. In 1996, it was estimated that some 2.6 million migrant workers were spread across Asia, from Singapore and Thailand to South Korea and Japan (Silverman 1996: 60–66). Some 20% of Singapore's labour force is made up of migrant workers, and the proportion is higher in Malaysia, where many illegal migrants swell the lower-paid end of the labour force. Amongst the exodus of migrant workers are large numbers of women from the Philippines, Indonesia, Sri Lanka and other Asian countries who go to the more affluent Asian countries (such as Singapore) to work as domestic maids. While earning much more than they could ever earn in their home countries (in Hong Kong SAR, Filipino maids can earn up to 15 times more than what they could earn at home), these maids are often subjected to harsh treatment, physical abuse, exploitation, sexual harassment, rape, and sometimes, murder (Rhodes 1993: 54–55). Leaving is not an easy option since in many countries, their employers keep their passports as security against them absconding with the family silver. Many of the women who go to other countries to work as maids leave their husbands and children behind. Apart from the emotional stress of not being able to see their families for long periods of time (often years), in several cases, these maids have discovered (usually through other women from their village who have come to work as maids) that in their absence, their husbands have acquired new wives and new children! Thus, the plight of women migrant workers in many Asian countries can be quite harrowing.

Perhaps the most graphic illustration of the lower status of women in Asian societies is their (often gross) under-representation in decision-making, either in business or in politics. In spite of being highly educated, Japanese women account for only 9% of business executives (compared to 44% in the USA, and 31% in Norway). In other Asian countries, the percentage of female business executives range from 4% in South Korea, to 38% in the Philippines. In politics, female members of parliament range from 1% in South Korea to 21% in China (United Nations Development Programme 1995: 60–62, 68–71). On the threshold of the 21st century, certain fundamentalist sections of India's predominantly Hindu society raised objections to the appointment of Mrs Sonja Gandhi as Prime Minister (because she was Italian born), should her Congress Party win the elections currently being held in that country. In Indonesia, certain Muslim groups raised objections to Mrs Megawati Sukarnoputri (whose party had won the general elections with over 30% of the vote) being elected President of the country because she was a woman.

Given societal attitudes towards women, and their role in many Asian societies, it is not very surprising that the share of resources devoted to their well-being is disproportionately less than their numbers in society. This is reflected in a number of indicators of female welfare. One example is the very high maternal mortality ratio in some countries, which is often associated with the very small proportion of births attended by skilled health staff. In Bangladesh and India, the maternal mortality ratio per 100,000 births during 1990–97 was 850 and 440 deaths, respectively. Over the same period of time, the percentage of births attended by skilled health staff was 8% in Bangladesh, and 35% in India. This is a reflection of the relative lack of resources devoted to womens' health in these countries. It is symptomatic of a mindset that is not restricted to poor countries. In 1998, the Japanese Ministry of Health approved the sale of contraceptives in Japan after deliberating on the matter for 30 years. In the same year, it had approved the sale of the anti-impotence drug, Viagra, after only a few months' consideration.

FROM EXTENDED TO NUCLEAR FAMILIES

Rural-urban migration

One of the significant developments in Asian (as well as many other less developed) countries since the 1950s has been the rapid growth of cities as a result of rural-urban migration. High rates of growth in rural areas, as well as much industrial and commercial development in and around cities, has resulted in large flows of people from rural to urban areas, in search of work and a better life.

As a consequence of this, urban population growth is often very much higher than the growth of the total population in many countries. Table 8.2 shows the relevant data. The table shows that, with rare exceptions, urban populations have been growing much faster than total populations in most Asian countries shown in the table. The highest rates of growth of urban populations are in Bangladesh, Indonesia, Philippines and Laos (about 5% per annum), but high rates of growth are also evident in other countries (for example, Cambodia, Malaysia and Pakistan). Except for the city states, between a quarter and about two-thirds of people live

in urban areas in most countries. Over 50% of the populations of
Malaysia and the Philippines live in urban areas. In South Korea,
the proportion is over 80%. The countries with the lowest rates of
urbanisation are in South Asia (Bangladesh), and in the former
Indo-Chinese states (Cambodia, Laos, Vietnam), but in many of
these countries, urban populations are increasing at a much faster
rate than the total population.

TABLE 8.2: TOTAL AND URBAN POPULATION GROWTH, 1980–2000, AND URBAN POPULATION/TOTAL POPULATION, 2000 (PER CENT)

Country	Total	Urban	%Urban
Bangladesh	2.1	4.9	25.0
India	2.0	3.0	28.0
Pakistan	2.6	4.1	37.0
Sri Lanka	1.4	1.8	24.0
Indonesia	1.7	4.9	41.0
Malaysia	2.6	4.3	57.0
Philippines	2.3	4.6	59.0
Thailand	1.3	2.6	22.0
Cambodia	2.8	4.4	16.0
Laos	2.5	5.6	24.0
Myanmar	1.7	2.5	28.0
Vietnam	1.9	3.0	24.0
Hong Kong SAR	1.5	2.0	100.0
Singapore	2.5	2.6	100.0
South Korea	1.1	2.9	82.0
China	1.3	3.8	32.0

Source: World Bank, *World Development Indicators 2002*

In many Asian countries, urban centres have grown so large
that they are now classified as "megacities" (defined as cities with
population sizes of 10 million people or more). Of the 15
megacities in the world in 1995, 10 were in Asia. These were
Jakarta, Karachi, Bombay, Delhi, Tianjin, Beijing, Shanghai,
Seoul, Calcutta, and Tokyo.

The trend toward nuclear families

One important consequence of rural-urban migration and rapid urbanisation is a shift from extended to nuclear families. As family members leave rural areas to seek work in the cities, the extended family system (where a large number of family members either live under the same roof, or live close to each other) breaks down. Often different family members migrate to different cities in search of work, but even when they go to the same city, shortages of space in urban areas often mean that they have to live apart from each other (United Nations Commission for Asia and the Pacific 1998: 73). This is most clearly seen in countries with high urbanisation rates (the city states, or South Korea, for example) where the acute shortage of space in cities, which has resulted in high-density living in small high-rise apartment blocks, has accentuated the trend toward nuclear familes. In Japan, the average household size declined from five persons in 1950 to three persons in 1985, while the proportion of extended family households fell from 36% in 1955 to 20% in 1985 (Mackerras 1995: 462, 464). In Hong Kong SAR, the mean household size has been declining by 24.4% per annum between 1970 and 1990, resulting in an average size of household of 3.4 persons in 1990. In South Korea, the decline in mean household size has been greater (28.8% per annum), resulting in an average household size of 3.7 persons in 1990. A smiliar trend can be observed for many other Asian countries since the 1980s (United Nations Commission for Asia and the Pacific 1998: 69–70).

THE WEAKENING OF THE FAMILY UNIT

The trend towards nuclear families and the withering of the extended family system has resulted in a number of social problems in many Asian countries. In times past, the extended family was an important source of emotional, physical and financial support for family members. People of all ages could rely on their family members to help them in times of stress and trouble. The young were looked after by older relatives, the aged were cared for by their children, and adults could always count on their extended family members for assistance and support in times of need.

With the gradual breakdown of the extended family system, these sources of support have all but disappeared in many Asian countries. Parents can no longer rely on their children for help, particularly when the latter have moved away. The aged have no one to care for them. In the cities, working parents have no one to help take care of their young children, who often wander the streets after school, or spend their time alone in their apartments watching television (Vatikiotis 1996: 38). In a recent survey taken in Hong Kong SAR, only 1.8% of respondents regarded relatives as trustworthy, and 34.6% disagreed or disagreed strongly that family members can be relied upon for help (Zeng and Wong 1999: 225).

The lack of family support and closeness has also contributed to increased youth delinquency. Children and adolescents spend less time with their parents or relatives, and more time in front of television sets. A survey of young people (aged 13 to 21 years) in Malaysia showed that 71% smoked cigarettes, 40% watched pornographic videos, 28% gambled, and 14% took hard drugs. In Jakarta and other large Indonesian cities, apparently unprovoked street fights (sometimes resulting in death) amongst gangs of school children are a frequent occurrence (Vatikiotis 1996: 39; Elegant 1996: 40–41).

MARRIAGE AND DIVORCE IN ASIAN SOCIETIES

Marriages

In many Asian countries, people (especially women rather than men) are getting married later in life, increasing proportions of both men and women prefer to remain single, and the incidence of divorce has been rising steadily over time.

In Hong Kong SAR, the mean age at marriage for females rose from 23.8 years in 1970 to 27.7 years in 1990, whilst that of males remained virtually unchanged at 30 years. In Thailand, the mean age at marrige for females rose from 24.3 years in 1970 to 27 years in 1990, while that of males rose from 27.8 years to 30 years. With rare exceptions, similar trends can be observed for other Asian countries (United Nations Commission for Asia and the Pacific 1998: 76–79). In Singapore, the mean age at marriage of men rose from 17 years in 1961 to 28.8 years in 1997, while that of women rose from 22 years to 26 years over the same period of time (Saw 1999: 104). The main reasons for this trend towards later marriage are increasing educational opportunities, as well as better employment opportunities. As people pursue higher educational qualifications, and concentrate on their professional careers, marriage tends to recede in their order of priorities.

In several countries, increasing proportions of people are choosing to remain single. Highly educated women, for example, often find it increasingly difficult to find suitable marriage partners. As a consequence of this, increasing numbers have remained unmarried. This is graphically illustrated in the case of Singapore. Table 8.3 shows the relevant data.

For all educational levels except below secondary, the percentage of women who are single (in all age groups) has risen significantly between 1980 and 1990. For example, in 1980, 5.7% of graduate women, aged 25–29 years remained unmarried, but by 1990, the proportion had risen to 11%. Many of these may be delaying the age of marriage, preferring to pursue their professional careers first. However, this is unlikely in the case of women in the 35–39 and 40+ age groups. In 1980, 13.2% of women aged 35–39 years with tertiary education (mainly Polytechnic and University graduates) remained unmarried. By 1990, the ratio had risen to 18.5%. Similarly for women aged 40 years and above, the proportion remaining unmarried increased from 5.6% to 12.6% between 1980 and 1990. For women in these age groups, it is as though having kissed frogs for years and finding that they did not change into handsome young princes, many of these women have given up on marriage and preferred to remain single.

TABLE 8.3: SINGLE FEMALES IN SINGAPORE BY EDUCATION AND AGE (PER CENT)

Education	Age (Years)				
	20–24	25–29	30–34	35–39	40+
1990					
Below Secondary	24.8	26.9	34.4	43.7	63.5
Secondary	42.4	44.5	42.5	37.7	23.9
Upper Sec/Poly	25.6	16.4	15.4	12.0	8.4
University	7.1	11.0	7.7	6.5	4.2
1980					
Below Secondary	57.5	60.8	65.0	67.9	86.4
Secondary	28.6	23.9	21.9	18.9	8.0
Upper Sec/Poly	11.3	9.6	8.7	9.4	4.0
University	2.6	5.7	4.4	3.8	1.6

Source: *Singapore Census of Population 1990* (Singapore: Department of Statistics)

The increasing proportions of educated women who remain unmarried are also a reflection of the fact that men often prefer to marry women who are less educated than themselves, while women often prefer not to marry men who are less educated than themselves. In other words, men prefer not to marry "up", and women prefer not to marry "down", as far as educational attainment is concerned. In 1997, 61.8% of graduate men married women with tertiary qualifications, while 38.2% married women with lower educational qualifications. On the other hand, 76.5% of graduate women married men with tertiary qualifications, while only 23.5% married men with lower educational qualifications (Saw 1999: 102).

One consequence of these trends is that, in Singapore, the rate of marriage (that is, marriages per thousand of population aged 15 years or more), declined steadily from 17.7 per thousand in 1973 to 10.7 per thousand in 1997 (Saw 1999: 94).

Divorces

With rapid economic growth, increasing educational and employment opportunities for women, legal protection of womens' rights, and changes in social attitudes, marriage breakdowns have been rising in many parts of Southeast and East Asia. Separation and divorce are becoming increasingly common, and no longer carry the social stigma that they once did. Women are far less financially dependent on men than they used to be, and much less willing to put up with unacceptable, abusive or violent behaviour from their spouses. As a consequence of this, rates of divorce have been rising in many Asian countries. Of every 1000 persons in Singapore in 1990, 1.3 suffered broken marriages (in 1980, the ratio was 0.7). In Malaysia, 909 divorce cases were processed by the courts in 1993 (up from 506 cases in 1980) (Vatikiotis 1996: 39).

FIGURE 8.2: DIVORCE RATES IN SINGAPORE AND CHINA, 1985–2000

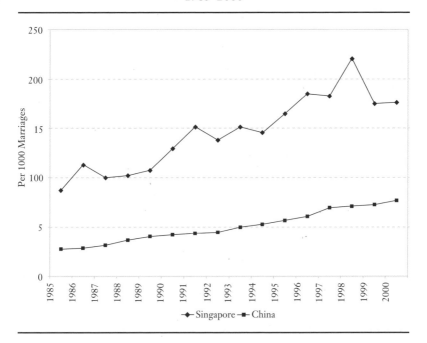

Source: Saw (1999), p. 117; State Statistical Bureau, *China Statistical Yearbook 2001*, p. 776

This general upward trend in divorces is shown in Figure 8.2, which shows the divorce rate (measured as the number of divorces per thousand marriages) in Singapore and China.

Figure 8.2 shows that in Singapore, the divorce rate has increased significantly between 1985 and 2000, more than doubling over this period of time. Divorce rates in China have been lower, but have also been increasing steadily over time, more than doubling between 1985 and 2000.

As a consequence of marital dissolution (as well as of other factors, such as widowhood), the percentage of female-headed households is quite high in some Asian countries. Data for the early 1990s show that 25.7% of households in Hong Kong SAR, and 18.2% of households in Singapore, were headed by females. Data for the early 1980s show that the percentages of households headed by females were 14.7% in South Korea, 16.5% in Thailand, and 16.8% in Bangladesh. These ratios are not very different from that of some developed countries such as Australia or New Zealand (United Nations Commission for Asia and the Pacific 1998: 73–75).

CONCLUSION

Although women make up approximately half the population, and often do most of the work (a large proportion of which is unpaid) in many societies, the resources devoted to their well-being often are not commensurate with their contribution to society. In terms of education, employment, remuneration, health, status, and treatment by society at large, or before the law, women in many Asian societies fare much worse than men. Although important strides have been made (especially in the Asian NICs, and in ASEAN countries) in many of these areas, the gender gap in many aspects of life is still quite wide in many Asian countries.

A general rise in education and employment opportunities in many parts of Asia has enabled many women to be financially less dependent on men, and enabled them to consider separation or divorce as alternatives to unhappy marriages. These options have, themselves, resulted in a number of social problems which have been compounded by a general trend away from extended to nuclear families.

PART 3

Political
Development

9

The Post-Colonial Era

INTRODUCTION

The end of the Second World War saw most of the countries of South, Southeast and East Asia gaining political independence. Some countries, like Indonesia and Vietnam, had to wrest their freedom from their colonial masters by driving them out through force of arms. Others, like India, Malaya and Singapore, were granted their independence without an armed struggle. They were decolonised.

THE STRUGGLE FOR INDEPENDENCE AND THE RISE OF COMMUNIST REGIMES

India and Pakistan

In South Asia, the beginning of political opposition to colonial rule and the exclusion of the local populace in political affairs, culminated in the formation of the Indian National Congress in 1885 (by Alan Hume, a former civil servant). Starting with demands for greater political freedoms (such as the right to elect provincial legislative councils), the Congress pressed for greater political reforms under its successive leaders. As the British grudgingly conceded limited local participation in central and regional political institutions, Congress stepped up its demands. These became more widespread and more strident after the 1919 Amristsar incident, when nearly 400 Indians were gunned down by British troops when they refused to disperse after a political rally.

Under the leadership of the charismatic Mohandas Karamchand Gandhi (1869–1948), Congress developed a policy of opposition to colonial rule through non-violent non-cooperation, and began a long struggle for independence based on civil disobedience. The British continued to resist this, offering to consider the granting of Dominion status in 1929 (this was rejected by Congress as inadequate), and granting increased autonomy to the provinces under the India Act of 1935.

The Second World War interrupted and delayed Indian nationalist aspirations for political independence. As in the First World War, Congress sided with the British in the hope of making the latter more amenable towards the granting of independence. The election of a socialist British Labour government after the war, under the Prime Ministership of Clement Atlee, marked a sea change in the British attitude toward the granting of independence to India. After a series of conferences, the British government announced in February 1947 that India would be granted independence. This occurred on August 15, 1947, but not without bloodshed as violent Hindu-Muslim rivalries resulted in the partition of the subcontinent into two separate states, India and Pakistan.

On gaining independence, India adopted a Prime Ministerial system of government based on the bi-cameral Westminster system. This has remained intact to this day, making India the world's largest democracy. Pakistan started with a similar system, but in 1958, the army Chief-of-Staff, General Mohamed Ayub Khan, seized power in a *coup d'etat*. This marked the start of a long period of military rule in Pakistan which ended in 1970, when the Pakistan Peoples' Party (under the leadership of Zulfikar Ali Bhutto) was swept into power in the country's first free elections.

Sri Lanka

When the British granted independence to India and Pakistan in 1947, they also made arrangements to grant independence to the island of Ceylon (now called Sri Lanka). This occurred on February 4, 1948, when Ceylon became an independent country within the British Commonwealth.

Ceylon inherited the British bicameral parliamentary system of democratic government and, in the first decade or so after independence, maintained close and friendly relations with

Britain. Until the early 1960s, the British continued to own most of the tea and coconut plantations, and to operate military bases on the island.

Tensions between the minority Hindu Tamils in the north and east of the island, and the Buddhist Singhalese in the south erupted in political violence in the late 1950s, when the government of Prime Minister Solomon Bandaranaike implemented nationalistic policies and made Singhalese the national language (replacing English). The Bandaranaike government also adopted socialist policies, cancelling defence arrangements with Britain, and nationalising basic industries.

In 1959, Prime Minister Bandaranaike was assassinated by a Buddhist fanatic, and was succeeded by his widow, Mrs Sirimavo Bandaranaike, who continued her late husband's nationalistic and socialist policies.

Burma

In Southeast Asia, the British had instituted political reforms in Burma as early as 1874 when municipal committees (nominated at first, elected later) were established in seven towns. From then on, the number of elected members in the various organs of government administration (such as the Legislative Council) were slowly increased. When Burma became a separate British colony in 1835, it was administered by a British governor, a Burmese Prime Minister, and a council of ten. By 1937, Burma had been given a large measure of self-government.

Burmese nationalism had started before the Second World War when the military commander, General Aung San, saw the invading Japanese as a means of forcing the British to grant his country independence. After the war, General Aung San negotiated a political settlement with the British, but before this could be put into effect, he was assassinated in July 1947 by his political enemies. U Nu, a founder of the Anti-Fascist People's Freedom League (AFPFL), took over leadership of the independence movement and won independence for his country in January 1948. Like India, Burma inherited the Westminster system of Prime Ministerial government. Constant infighting between rival factions in the AFPFL resulted in internal political instability. In March 1962, General Ne Win seized power in a *coup d'etat*, plunging Burma into a long period of military dictatorship which persists to this day.

Malaya

As in other parts of Southeast Asia, British colonial rule in Malaya was interrupted by the Japanese occupation during the Second World War. After the war, the British returned to pick up where they had left off. Late in 1945, the British formed the Malayan Union which comprised Penang, Malacca and the nine Malay states. Singapore remained a separate crown colony. The Malayan Union was opposed by the newly formed United National Malay Organisation (UMNO) and its charismatic leader, Dato Onn Bin Jaffar, who feared that the rights of the Malays would be eroded. It was later replaced by a federation of Malay states. During this period, the two other major racial groups in Malaya, the Chinese and the Indians, formed their own political parties (the Malayan Chinese Association and the Malayan Indian Congress) to safeguard the rights of their communities. These three major political parties joined forces in an Alliance Party in order to press for independence from Britain. After protracted negotiations during the 1950s, Malaya was granted independence in August 1957. Its first Prime Minister, the aristocratic Tengku Abdul Rahman (who had taken over the leadership of UMNO) inherited a Westminster form of government that was common to many former British colonies. Singapore, Sarawak and North Borneo remained British colonies until 1963, when after a long political struggle with the Communists, they were merged into the expanded federation of Malaysia. Singapore's tenure in the Malaysian federation was short-lived. In 1965, after irreconcilable political differences with the UMNO-dominated Alliance Party threatened to break out in widespread communal violence, it was forced to leave the federation and begin its life as an independent island state.

Although both Malaysia and Singapore inherited the Westminster model of democratic government, the British legal system and the rule of law, both countries have been ruled by one political party since independence. In Malaysia, UMNO has held power (through first the Alliance Party, and then the National Front) since independence was attained in 1957. In Singapore, the Peoples' Action Party has held power since 1959 when the island state was first granted internal self-government.

Indonesia

Like the British, the Dutch returned to Indonesia after the Second World War, hoping to pick up where they had left off. A few months before the Japanese surrendered, a Republic of Indonesia had already been proclaimed by the Independence Preparatory Committee on August 17, 1945. The charismatic Sukarno was named President with Mohamed Hatta as his Vice-President. When the Dutch returned to Indonesia at the end of 1945, they tried to reimpose colonial rule over the archipelago. The Indonesians reacted with armed resistance, and in 1947 and 1948, the Dutch mounted a series of "police actions" against Indonesian freedom fighters.

In 1949, the United Nations Security Council passed a resolution in favor of transferring sovereignty to a United States of Indonesia. Under pressure from the United States, the Dutch conceded and on December 27, 1949, recognised the independence of the Republic of the United States of Indonesia. The following year, on August 17, 1950, the federal system of government was transformed into a unitary state, with Sukarno as its President.

Internal dissent in Indonesia became more pronounced after independence as the outer islands became more and more disenchanted with the dominance of Java and the Javanese in Indonesian political affairs. At the same time, political unrest had been fermented by the Communists led by its charismatic leader, D. N. Aidit. In 1956, regional army commanders in Sumatra proclaimed independence, sparking off fears of a prolonged civil war. In 1957, President Sukarno announced his programme of "Guided Democracy", and within a few months of this, declared martial law. In 1959, the elected constituent was dissolved, and Indonesia began a long period of authoritarian rule. This continued after Sukarno's downfall in 1965 after a failed *coup d'etat*. His successor, President Suharto, proclaimed a "New Order" in which his authoritarian rule was entrenched.

In May 1998, following the collapse of the Indonesian economy as a result of the Asian currency crisis, President Suharto was forced to step down. His Vice-President, the unpopular Dr B. J. Habibie took over as President. The first free general elections since 1955 were held in July 1999. In November 1999, Abdurraman Wahid was elected President of the Republic of Indonesia, with Megawati Sukarnoputri as its Vice-president. This marked the beginning of Indonesia's transition from authoritarianism to democracy.

Philippines

Spain lost control over its colony in the Philippines in 1898 after it was defeated by the Americans in the Spanish-American War. Nationalist pressures for independence had already begun during the decades prior to the Spanish defeat. Jose Rizal (1861–1896) had been highly critical of Spanish rule, and was executed in 1896 for instigating rebellion. With the defeat of the Spanish, exiled nationalist leaders returned to the Philippines. Amongst these was Emilo Aguinaldo who proclaimed an independent Philippine Republic on June 12, 1898.

The Americans, intent on securing their newly-found possession, occupied Manila on August 13, 1898, sparking off an armed conflict with pro-independence fighters led by Aguinaldo. By 1901, the Americans had subdued armed resistance and the Philippines passed into a period under American rule.

During periods in which the Democratic Party held power in Washington, the Americans prepared the Philippines for eventual independence, establishing the various organs of government such as the Senate, the Assembly and the Council of State. In 1934, the passage of the Tydings-McDuffie Act promised independence to the Philippines after a ten-year transitional period of self-rule, during which external affairs would be controlled by the Americans. The following year, Manuel Quezon was elected President of the Philippine Commonwealth government, with Sergio Osmena as his Vice-President.

The Philippines progress to full independence was interrupted by the Second World War when it was occupied by the Japanese. After the war ended, the Americans returned and granted independence to the Philippines on July 4, 1946. By this time, a new President, Manual Roxas, had been elected, but he died only after two years in office and was succeeded by his Vice-President, Elpido Quirino.

The Philippines inherited an American-style presidential form of government, and is reputed to be one of the most democratic countries in Southeast and East Asia.

INDOCHINA

Vietnam

After the Second World War, the French attempted to return to Indochina and to reimpose their colonial rule. While they re-occupied the south of Vietnam with relative ease (setting up a puppet government under Bao Dai in the process), they encountered stiff resistance in the north, where Ho Chi Minh had set up the Democratic Republic of Vietnam in 1946. Although this was recognised by the French as a free state within the French Union, hostilities broke out and then escalated between the two parties. In November 1946, the French bombed the city port of Haiphong killing many thousands of people. In December, the Ho Chi Minh's forces attacked the French in Hanoi. This was the start of the Vietnam War that was to last seven and a half years.

The French were eventually defeated in 1954 when their forces surrendered to General Vo Nguyen Giap (one of the most brilliant military minds of this century) at Bien Ben Phu. By this time, however, the United States had become increasingly involved in Vietnam, first by providing aid and military advisors to the south, and later by intervening in the war. As a result of the Geneva Conference of 1954, Vietnam was partitioned into North Vietnam (above the 17th parallel) and South Vietnam.

In 1955, Ngo Dinh Diem was installed as President of the Republic of South Vietnam after deposing Bao Dai. Fearing that all of Southeast Asia could come under Communist rule if South Vietnam fell (the "domino theory"), the USA increased its involvement in fighting the Vietcong, pouring men and money into the war effort. After several *coups d'etat* in which a succession of South Vietnamese generals took over the leadership of the country, and the loss of many American lives, the USA finally abandoned South Vietnam in 1975.

The end of the Vietnam War in 1975 led to the reunification of the country under Communist rule. The government immediately began the reconstruction of the economy, imposing a Soviet-type centrally-planned economic system. By the mid-1980s, the gross inefficiencies of such a system of economic organisation was plain to see, and the government implemented a series of market-oriented economic reforms, under the banner of *doi moi* (economic renovation). As in China, these reforms effectively dismantled the system of central planning, and provided material incentives aimed at boosting agricultural and industrial production.

By the early 1980s, Vietnam had implemented a (largely) market-oriented economic system, and opened its doors to international trade and investment. Its rate of economic growth and development soared, as export-oriented manufacturing firms were attracted to its low-cost labour.

Like China, economic liberalisation in Vietnam was not accompanied by political reforms. The Communist Party kept its firm grip on political power, resisting calls for greater political freedoms.

Laos

After the Second World War, the French also attempted to return to Laos to pick up where they had left off before the war. Disagreement between King Sisavang Vong and his Prime Minister (and eldest son), Prince Phetsarath on whether to allow the French to return led to the establishment of the Free Lao (Lao Issarak) movement, a declaration of independence, the deposing of the king, and the formation of a provisional government led by Prince Souvanna Phouma and Prince Souphanouvong (half-brother of the former). In 1945, the French responded by taking the country by force and reinstating the king. The leaders of the Free Lao movement went into exile.

In 1949, the French gave Laos self-government within the French Union. This led to the dissolution of the Free Lao movement, and the return of its leaders (except Prince Phetsarath) from exile. The Laotian government was headed by Prince Souvanna Phouma, but was controlled by the French. Both the French and the government of Prince Souvanna Phouma (a neutralist) were opposed by the Communist Pathet Lao, led by Prince Souphanouvong. By 1954, the Pathet Lao controlled Phong Saly and Sam Neua, two northern provinces of the country.

The French defeat at Dien Bien Phu, and their subsequent withdrawal from Indochina, left Laos an independent, undivided country. Although the 1954 Geneva Convention tried to ensure its independence, unity and neutrality, the struggle for power between leftists (led by Prince Souphanouvong), and rightists (led by Phoui Sananikone, who succeeded Prince Souvanna Phouma as Prime Minister), led to escalating political instability. In 1960, a *coup d'etat* was staged by Kong Le, who announced the formation of a neutralist government under Prince Souvanna Phouma. When open hostilities broke out between the rightists and the neutralists, Prince Souvanna Phouma fled to the north of the country to join forces with his half-brother, Prince Souphanouvong.

A civil war broke out between leftist and rightist forces in 1963. By this time, Cold War politics had entered the fray, with the USA supporting first, Prince Souvanna Phouma, and then Prince Boun Oum (who had been named Prime Minister of a rightist government in 1961). The Pathet Lao (led by Prince Souphanouvong), on the other hand, were supported by the Soviet

Union and North Vietnam. This brought Laos in to the Vietnam War as the US started to bomb suspected Vietcong supply routes on the Lao side of the border.

The Communist victory in Vietnam in 1975, and the withdrawal of US forces from Indochina, also resulted in a Communist victory in Laos. As in Vietnam, the Communist government set about the establishment of a Soviet-type, centrally-planned economy in Laos. By 1979, increasing peasant opposition and declining output forced the government to implement a series of market-oriented economic reforms in agriculture, as well as in industry. By 1989, this had been extended to include privatisation of state-owned enterprises. By the mid-1990s, Laos had all but abandoned central-planning.

Cambodia

When the French returned to Cambodia in 1945, they put an end to a budding movement for independence by arresting Son Ngoc Thanh who had been appointed Prime Minister by King Norodom Sihanouk only months earlier. The French gave Cambodia limited self-government, but still controlled foreign affairs, defence, internal security, and the judiciary. In early 1953, King Sihanouk started pressing for independence, garnering support from major Western powers such as the USA. By the middle of the year, *de facto* recognition of Cambodia as an independent state was achieved.

In 1955, King Sihanouk abdicated (his father became King) in order to participate in the political process. His political party was swept into power in the 1955 general elections. In foreign affairs, Prince Sihanouk followed a path of neutrality, switching from pro-Western to pro-Communist policies (and vice versa), as the situation required. In the late 1960s, Cambodia was drawn into the Vietnam War as the US began to bomb northeastern Cambodia in an effort to disrupt Communist supply routes passing through that region. The Communists had also used sanctuaries in eastern Cambodia for storing supplies and as the base of the guerrilla movement, the Central Office for South Vietnam (COSVN).

About the same time, the Khmer Rouge (Cambodian Communists) began to increase their activities. They were disbanded in 1954, and had split into two factions (one pro-Hanoi and based in North Vietnam, the other anti-Hanoi and based in Cambodia). In the late 1960s, the Cambodian faction of the Khmer Rouge, led by Pol Pot, started a campaign of guerrilla warfare against the Sihanouk government.

In 1970, whilst Prince Sihanouk was on an overseas trip, his Prime Minister, General Lol Nol (an anti-Communist) seized power in a *coup d'etat*. Learning of this, Prince Sihanouk fled to Beijing where he was granted political asylum. Lon Nol, supported by the USA, moved against the Communists, starting a civil war in the process.

The withdrawal of American forces in 1975 meant the end of the Lon Nol government which was defeated by the Khmer Rouge (backed by China) a month before the fall of Saigon. The Khmer Rouge, under Pol Pot, waged a reign of terror, emptying the cities and killing over a million people in the process.

The genocidial rule of the Khmer Rouge came to an end in 1978, when Vietnam (backed by the Soviet Union) invaded Cambodia, forcing Pol Pot and his followers into the jungle. A long period of internal warfare ensued.

In 1991, the Cambodian problem was solved with the signing of the Paris Conference of Cambodia agreements. General elections were held under the auspices of the United Nations, but the Khmer Rouge refused to participate. Neither FUNCINPEC (the party of Prince Ranariddh, son of Prince Sihanouk), nor the Cambodian Peoples' Party (or CPP, led by Hun Sen) won a clear majority. A coalition government was formed, with Prince Sihanouk as Head of State and Premier. Prince Ranarriddh and Hun Sen were named as coequal Deputy Premiers.

Tensions between Prince Ranariddh and Hun Sen continued to simmer over a long period of time. Meanwhile, the Khmer Rouge, which had retreated to the jungles in the north of the country, had begun to splinter into factions, many deserting or surrendering to the government. The death (some claimed he committed suicide) of Pol Pot in 1997, brought an end to the Khmer Rouge as a force in Cambodian politics. In 1997, Hun Sen staged a *coup d'etat*, forcing Prince Ranariddh into exile. With the last remaining serious challenge to his power removed, Hun Sen assumed total power in Cambodia.

After the Vietnamese invasion of Cambodia, the government (with the help of Vietnamese advisors) attempted to establish a Soviet-type, centrally-planned economic system. This was not entirely successful as individual production, private land-use rights, and free markets were allowed. By the late 1980s, these were confirmed by new laws on land reform. Although in theory, all land belongs to the state, this is not enforced in practice. In industry, a number of market-oriented economic reforms were implemented after 1985, virtually dismantling the centrally-planned system. State-owned enterprises were privatised (mainly through leasing arrangements), and foreign investment was encouraged through the passing of a Foreign Investment Law in 1989. By the early 1990s, Cambodia (like other former Indo-Chinese countries) had virtually abandoned Communist forms of economic organisation.

China

In 1949, after a bloody civil war, the Chinese Communist Party, led by Chairman Mao Zedong, defeated the Nationalists led by Generalissimo Chiang Kai Shek, who fled with his Kuomintang Party followers to the island of Taiwan.

The Communists lost no time in reshaping the Chinese economy. After a brief period (1949–52) of reconstruction (from the devastations of the war with Japan, and the civil war), they undertook a major reform of the economy during the First Five Year Plan (1953–57). With help from the Soviet Union, a Soviet-type, centrally-planned economy was established. By the end of the First Five Year Plan, Chairman Mao had grown increasingly unhappy with Soviet-type heavy industry development and its consequent neglect of agriculture.

In 1958, following the Sino-Soviet split, Chairman Mao launched the Great Leap Forward (1958–60) which was aimed at

reversing some of the more unpalatable aspec
model of development. This proved to be a cata
weather and gross mismanagement of the econor
scale famine, in which some 30 million people wer
have perished.

A period of reconstruction and reform (1961–6ɔ) ensued as
market-oriented economic reforms were implemented under the
leadership of Liu Shaoqi and Deng Xiaoping in a bid to provide the
material incentives required to stimulate production. This alarmed
conservatives in the Communist Party (including Mao himself) who
feared a return of capitalism.

In 1966, Chairman Mao launched the Great Proletarian Cultural
Revolution (1966–76), in which all traces of "right wing" tendencies
were to be removed from society. With the help of the fanatical "Red
Guards" and the "Gang of Four" (of which his wife, Jiang Qing, was
the leader), Chairman Mao unleashed a reign of terror on his people
and brought the Chinese economy to its knees.

The death of Chairman Mao in September 1976 brought an
end to the Cultural Revolution, and after a brief interregnum, Deng
Xiaoping assumed the paramount leadership of the country. The
Red Guards were disbanded and the Gang of Four were arrested.
Starting from 1978, a series of market-oriented economic reforms
were implemented in agriculture, industry, trade and investment,
opening the country up, for the first time in half a century, to the
outside world. This led to rapid economic growth and
development, first in the southern provinces adjacent to Hong
Kong SAR and Taiwan, but later spreading inland. By the late
1980s, China had emerged as one of the economic powerhouses of
Asia, taking its place as one of the most important producers and
exporters of manufactured goods. By this time, China had, for all
intents and purposes, embraced capitalism inspite of its large state-
owned sector.

The market-oriented economic reforms implemented after the
death of Chairman Mao were not accompanied by political reforms.
Unlike the Soviet Union, China liberalised its economic system,
but not its political system. The Communist Party, led by Deng

᛭iaoping (who died in February 1997) and his successor, Jiang Zemin, kept its iron grip on political power, suppressing political dissent, often ruthlessly (as in the case of the Tiananmen Massacre in 1989). Many political dissidents were sent to labour camps, or to exile in foreign countries. Ten years later, its suppression of the Falungong movement underlined its continued determination to curb any challenges (however far-fetched) to its monopoly over political power.

Korea

At the end of the Second World War, the Allies had to decide what to do with Korea which Japan had annexed in 1910. As early as August 1945, the USA had decided to partition Korea at the 38th parallel, just north of its capital Seoul. The reason for this was the expectation that the Soviet Union would occupy the north of the peninsula. It therefore seemed prudent that the USA should seek a partition of the country and occupy the south.

Shortly after the Japanese formally surrendered on August 15, 1945, the Koreans established the Korean Peoples' Republic with its capital in Seoul, but this was later declared unlawful by US troops which landed at Inchon in September, and established military rule.

By the end of the year, a Representative Democratic Council had been formed, with Syngman Rhee as its chairman. In the north, Kim Il Sung was declared leader with the support of the Red Army. In December, the North Korean People's Interim Committee was set up with Kim Il Sung as its chairman. These developments cast the die which made reunification of the country virtually impossible.

In 1948, a UN-sponsored general election in the south resulted in the election of Syngman Rhee as president of the newly established Republic of South Korea. This brought an end of US military rule. The Rhee administration was corrupt and unpopular. Between 1946 and 1950, the south was racked by peasant uprisings and industrial disputes. In the north, a general election was held. It was won by Kim Il Sung and his Worker's Party. On September 2, 1948, a Supreme

People's Assembly elected Kim Il Sung as Premier and Head of State of the Democratic People's Republic of Korea (which was established one week later).

On June 25, 1950, following escalating tensions between the north and the south, China-backed North Korean forces attacked US-backed South Korean forces, starting the Korean War. As a result of US pressure in the Security Council (which the Soviet Union had boycotted because of the UN's failure to admit China), a UN force under the command of US General MacArthur was formed to assist South Korea. The Korean War ended in July 1953 when an armistice was signed. However, the war was never formally ended and a peace agreement was never signed.

After the end of the Korean War, a tense peace settled over the peninsula. Forays by North Korean forces into the south were frequent events, even in the late 1990s. South Korea adopted a free-market, capitalist economic system, while North Korea became a Soviet-type, centrally-planned economy. In the late 1990s, when most former Communist countries in Eastern Europe, Southeast and East Asia had abandoned central planning, North Korea remained one of the two countries in the world which had not done so (the other is Cuba). The death of Kim Il Sung in 1994 did not change this.

COMMUNIST INSURGENCIES

Shortly after having attained political independence, several Southeast Asian countries in which Communists had not attained power, were faced with armed Communist, or Communist-inspired, insurgencies. Many of these had their beginnings during the Japanese occupation when they waged guerrilla warfare against Japanese troops. Some were promised full recognition as legitimate participants in the political process once the Japanese had been defeated. When such promises were not kept, these groups resorted to an armed struggle against the newly independent authorities. Others had been infiltrated by Communists during the Second World War. With the end of hostilities, they continued the pursuit of their aims.

Philippines

In the Philippines, the Hukbalahaps (or Huks, for short) were established in 1942 as an anti-Japanese army just before Philippines and American forces surrendered to the Japanese. During their subsequent armed resistance against the Japanese, the Huks were infiltrated by Communists. After the war, the Huks, having been prevented from taking up the six Congressional seats which they had won in the 1946 general elections, led an agrarian uprising in Central Luzon and carried on guerrilla warfare against the Quirino and Magsaysay administrations. Magsaysay, in his role as Secretary of Defence in the Quirino government, eventually suppressed the Huk rebellion by offering a general amnesty, 25 acres of land and a house, to those who gave up the armed struggle. In the process, he also managed to decimate the leadership and the top echelons of the Communist Party. By the early 1950, the Huks had become a spent force even though remnants of their number continued their armed struggle against the government.

The Communist Party of the Philippines soon regrouped and re-launched its armed struggle (by then, against the Marcos administration) with the establishment of the New Peoples' Army (NPA). In 1997, its leader, Jose Maria Sison, was captured and in the following year, most of the party's top leadership had either been killed or captured. This did not prevent the NPA from continuing to pursue its goal of overthrowing the government.

Malaya

In British Malaya, the colonial government hastily forged an agreement with the Malayan Communist Party to train guerrilla fighters as the Japanese army swept through Thailand and the northern states of the Malay federation in 1941. These fighters later formed the core of the Malayan People's Anti-Japanese Army (MPAJA). During the Japanese occupation of Malaya, the British formed Force 136 whose members were dropped behind enemy lines in order to organise and train guerrilla fighters against the Japanese. Amongst their number was Chin Peng, who was later to become the leader of the Malayan Communist Party (MCP), and who was, after the war, decorated by the British for his role in helping to defeat the Japanese.

After the war, the Communists decided to work with other political interests in a united front in order to achieve political independence for Malaysia. This took the form of the Malayan Democratic Union which was formed in Singapore at the end of 1945. The Communists also infiltrated the trade unions and Chinese-medium schools so that they could create industrial and social unrest in support of their political demands. The colonial government quickly recognised the Malayan Democratic Union as little more than a Communist-front organisation and took all necessary steps to counter its influence. In 1948, the government banned any federation of labour unions that were not associated with trade, and decreed that trade union officials had to have at least three years' experience in labour organisations. In addition, the government had the means to deport any Chinese not born in Malaya to China (and to almost certain death as China was then controlled by the Kuomintang). When three European plantation managers were killed by Communist guerrillas in June 1948, a State of Emergency was declared. One of its provisions was to give the government the power of detention without trial. At the same time, the Malayan Communist Party was banned. This eventually led to the dissolution of the Malayan Democratic Union.

The failure of the united front policy resulted in the Communists retreating into the jungles of Malaya to pursue their goals through an armed struggle which was to last many years and to cost many lives. By 1960, the MCP had, for all intents and purposes, been defeated. Chin Peng and the remnants of his guerrilla band fled to the jungles of southern Thailand where they continued to launch periodic attacks on government security forces. Even though the Malayan Emergency had been officially declared over in 1960, it was not until the early 1990s that Chin Peng and his band of (by now) aged revolutionaries finally gave up the struggle. With the death of Chairman Mao in 1976, the implementation of market-oriented reforms soon after, and the collapse of Communism in 1989 (epitomised by the dismantling of the Berlin Wall in that year), Chin Peng finally gave up the struggle and retired to China. Whilst some of his followers accompanied him, many were re-integrated into Malaysian society. Not only had the MCP failed to galvanise local support for its ideals, but international support had also petered out.

CONCLUSION

After the end of the Second World War, many countries in South, Southeast, and East Asia attained independence from their former colonial masters. Some had to fight to oust the returning colonial powers, whilst others were given their independence voluntarily.

After gaining their independence, some countries adopted democratic forms of government, whilst others (often after a protracted struggle) established Communist regimes. Several degenerated into military dictatorships, or authoritarian one-party regimes. By the late 1980s however, almost all countries in the region (even Communist ones) had adopted market-oriented economic systems. The collapse of Communism in 1989 led to the abandonment of central planning by most Communist regimes in Southeast and East Asia.

In countries which had adopted democratic forms of government, Communist insurgencies broke out in the 1950s. However, none of those was successful, and by the late 1980s (or early 1990s), Communism was no longer a potent force in the politics of these countries.

10

The Rise of Authoritarian States

INTRODUCTION

Many countries in Asia which started out as independent, sovereign, democratic states after the end of the Second World War, later became authoritarian, one-party states. Some became military dictatorships. In some countries, these forms of government persisted until the 1990s. In others, popular pressures for political reforms led to a process of democratisation, in several cases, leading to popularly elected governments.

AUTHORITARIAN STATES IN ASIA

South Asia

As mentioned in the previous chapter, Pakistan started, in 1949, as a liberal democracy under the leadership of Mohamed Jinna, its first Governor General. Its initial attempts at democracy were characterised by rampant corruption and ineffective government. Democratic government in Pakistan came to an abrupt end in 1958 when General Ayub Khan seized power in a *coup d'etat*, and imposed martial law. The usual reasons for a military takeover were given — incompetence of politicians, widespread corruption, the weakening of national institutions, and the imminent collapse of the state. He transformed Pakistan into a republic and was elected President. However, his authoritarian rule provoked much opposition and social unrest. In 1969, he stepped down and was replaced by another military leader, General Yahya Khan, who continued the authoritarian rule of his predecessor.

At its inception, Pakistan had been made up of two parts, East Pakistan and West Pakistan, separated by nearly 2,000 kilometres of Indian territory. East Pakistan had always felt unhappy with the fact that it was under-represented in the national government, and that its language, Bengali, was not recognised as a national language (General Ayub Khan had made Urdu, spoken in West Pakistan, the national language). In 1970, general elections were held, and the East Pakistan Party was returned on a platform of greater autonomy for East Pakistan. General Yahya Khan responded by sending in the Pakistani Army, sparking off a civil war. India soon intervened, defeating the Pakistani Army and leading to the creation of a new independent state in the sub-continent, Bangladesh.

The loss of East Pakistan led to General Yahya Khan's political demise. In Pakistan (now comprised only of the former West Pakistan), parliamentary democracy returned under the Prime Ministership of Zulfikar Ali Bhutto. Again, rampant corruption and political intrigue led to another *coup d'etat*, this time by General Zia-ul-Haq (who subsequently put Bhutto to death for the alleged murders of political opponents). General Zia's harsh authoritarian rule was cut short when he died in an aeroplane crash in 1988. In November of that year, general elections swept Benazir Bhutto (daughter of Zulfikar Ali Bhutto) into power. Since then, Pakistan has been ruled alternatively by Benazir Bhutto or her arch-rival, Nawaz Sharif. Democratic government returned to Pakistan after decades of military dictatorship, but corruption and gross mismanagement of the economy has remained a feature of national life, irrespective of the party or Prime Minister in power.

On October 13, 1999, Prime Minister Nawaz Sharif sacked the Army Chief of Staff, General Parvez Musharraf, who responded by staging a *coup d'etat*, dismissing the government and placing the Prime Minister under house arrest. Once again, a democratically-elected government in Pakistan had been deposed in a bloodless coup, and the country entered another period of military rule. In 26 of the 50 years since its creation as a nation state, Pakistan has been ruled by military dictatorships.

170

In Bangladesh, separation from Pakistan in 1971 brought Sheik Mujibur Rahman to power. Within a few years (in 1974), Sheik Mujibur Rahman was killed by his own army. His government had been riddled with corruption and nepotism. A series of coups and counter-coups ensued, leading eventually to the establishment of a three-man martial law administration led by General Ziaur Rahman, who assumed the Presidency in 1977. General Ziaur Rahman was assassinated in 1981, and replaced by General H. M. Ershad who took over the Presidency in 1983. Until he was deposed in 1990, General Ershad ruled Pakistan with an iron fist, declaring a state of emergency and dissolving parliament. A general election, held in 1991, swept Khaleda Zia (wife of the former President, General Ziaur Rahman) into power. Since then, Bangladesh has been ruled, alternatively, by Khaleda Zia and her nemesis, Sheikh Hasina Wajed (daughter of the first Prime Minster of Bangladesh, Sheikh Mujibur Rahman).

For most of the second half of the twentieth century, Pakistan and Bangladesh have been ruled, for long periods of time, by military dictatorships. On the sub-continent, only India has maintained a democratic form of government. Although the Congress Party was in power for decades (between 1949 and 1996, it was not in power for only four years), political power is contestable through the ballot box in India and it remains the world's largest democracy.

Although Sri Lanka (its new name was adopted in 1972) started its post-independent history as a parliamentary democracy, it soon descended into a one-party state under the leadership of the Bandaranaikes. Since independence, Sri Lanka has been ruled by one party, the Sri Lankan Freedom Party, and virtually by one family (the Bandaranaike family) for much of its post-war history.

Like many other Asian countries, it continued to maintain the outward trappings of a democratic state while real power was firmly entrenched in the hands of the Freedom Party and its leaders. Through the politics of corruption, patronage and violence, the Freedom Party has ruled Sri Lanka for most of its post-independence history. A political dynasty has also emerged. Not only was Prime Minister Solomon Bandaranaike succeeded by his wife, but their daughter, Mrs Kumaratunga is now President of Sri Lanka. One of her first acts as President was to appoint her mother as Prime Minister.

A long period of discrimination against the large Tamil minority in the north and east of the island erupted in civil war in 1983, when the Liberation Tigers of Tamil Eelam (LTTE) took up arms against the central government in a bid to establish an independent Tamil state in the north.

A long civil war ensued, with many tens of thousands of people killed, not only because of the armed conflict, but also because of Tamil suicide bombers.

By the early 1990s, it was clear to both sides that a military solution to the conflict was not possible, and moves were made to move towards a political solution. In early 2000, negotiations between the Sri Lankan government and the LTTE took place in Thailand. Both sides agreed to an end to hostilities and to work towards an agreement in which the Tamils of the north and east of the island would be granted autonomy within the Sri Lankan state.

Southeast Asia

Burma started life as an independent country under the leadership of Prime Minster U Nu (the leader of Burmese independence, General Aung San, had been assassinated in 1947 by a political rival, U Saw). A bicameral system of government had been adopted. U Nu's party won the general elections of 1951 and 1956 with overwhelming support. In 1962, General Ne Win seized power in a *coup d'etat* and established a repressive military dictatorship over Burma that was to last a quarter of a century.

In 1988, large scale popular protests against the military regime led to a brutal repression, resulting in the loss of many thousands of lives. General Ne Win resigned, but his Burma Socialist Program Party held on to the reins of power under the leadership of his stalwarts. In anticipation of a change in the political landscape of the country, a number of new political parties were formed, amongst them, the National League for Democracy

(NLD) led by (amongst others), Aung San Suu Kyi (daughter of General Aung San), and the Democracy and Peace Interim League led by U Nu and other national leaders. On September 9, 1988, U Nu announced the formation of a provisional government.

The military leaders responded by dismissing the President, and setting up a new government on September 24, 1988. Real power was in the hands of the State Law and Order Restoration Council (SLORC), led by General Saw Maung and which included most of Burma's regional military commanders and other high-ranking military officers. Although the NLD won the general elections in 1990, it was not allowed to form a new government and Aung San Suu Kyi was placed under house arrest.

So, for most of its post-colonial history, Burma (whose name was changed by the SLORC to Myanmar in 1989) has been ruled by a military dictatorship. Its long record of human rights abuses and suppression of democratic freedoms, has earned it an unenviable reputation as one of the pariah states of the world.

At the the end of the Second World War, parliamentary democracy was restored to Thailand (ending a long period of military rule after a *coup d'etat* in 1932), when general elections were held in 1946, and Pridi Phanamyong became Prime Minister under a new constitution. Political instability ensued as a small elite jockeyed for positions of power, and several administrations came and went in rapid succession.

In 1948, a *coup d'etat* brought Thailand under military rule once again, this time under a triumvirate led by Phibun Songkhram. This lasted until 1957 when general elections were held, and Phibun's party was returned with a large majority. Allegations of electoral fraud, and increasing dissension between Phibun and one of his previous coup partners, Sarit Thanarat, led to the latter staging a *coup d'etat* against Phibun in 1957. In 1963, another military commander, Thanom Kittikachorn, took over the reins of power when Sarit Thanarat died. By 1973, Thailand's increasing involvement in the Vietnam War as an ally of the USA and its military dictatorship had bred strong resentment, especially amongst university students. Widespread student protests in October 1973 led to the deaths of many people. This led to the King intervening by dismissing Kittikachorn and his deputy, Prapas Charusathien, and appointing Sanya Thammasak (rector of Thammasat University) to become Prime Minister. Political instability ensued as rightists and leftists vied for power. Prime Ministers and governments came and went as violent demonstrations erupted. In February 1991, another military coup brought an end to civilian rule as the army took over power once again, this time, under the leadership of a six-man junta controlled by Suchinda Kraprayoon. A civilian government under the Prime Ministership of the much-respected Anand Punyarachun was appointed by the military junta. A new constitution was adopted and general elections were held in 1992. This did not produce a clear majority for any party. When Suchinda Kraprayoon was nominated as Prime Minister by pro-military parties (even though he had not been elected to parliament), widespread protests broke out on the streets of Bangkok. On May 19, many demonstrators were killed by the military and many more were injured. The King intervened once again, forcing Suchinda Kraprayoon to step down as Prime Minister. New elections were held the following year, bringing the much-respected Chuan Leekpai into power.

Between 1932 and 1968, Thailand had 26 *coups d'etat*, 31 changes of government, and eight constitutions. This record continued until 1992, with more military coups, new constitutions and frequent changes of government. This is a reflection of the intense competition for political power between the military, the bureaucracy, and a small elite of aristocrats and professionals. For much of its post-war history, weak coalitions, political instability, corruption and electoral fraud have given the military the excuse they needed to seize power.

In 1957, President Sukarno enunciated his concept of "Guided Democracy" in which government by majority rule would be replaced by government by mutual consensus. In practice, Indonesia would be ruled by a personal dictatorship that was to last until 1965. Martial law was proclaimed. The pretext for President Sukarno's monopolisation of the levers of power was that the country needed to be rescued from the political (and economic) abyss to which it was rapidly descending. Between 1949 and 1955, Indonesia (under the leadership of President Sukarno) attempted to establish a parliamentary democracy. This proved to be very difficult. The first general election in 1955 resulted in a large number of parties each winning a few seats. None had a majority, or a mandate, to form a government. Five cabinets were formed and dismissed in six years. Democracy did not appear to be working in Indonesia. It needed to be "guided".

The early years of independence were turbulent years for the new Indonesian republic. Persistent internal political instability was accompanied by a rapidly deteriorating economy caused by gross mismanagement. In 1956, regional military commanders in Sumatra rebelled and proclaimed independence. Two years later, a revolutionary government was set up. The irredentist movement was crushed by loyal military commanders in 1961. In 1962, Indonesia invaded Dutch New Guinea (now known as Irian Jaya), eventually persuading the United Nations to recognise it as part of the Indonesian republic. The next year, President Sukarno launched his policy of Konfrontasi against the newly-formed Federation of Malaysia, bringing Indonesia into armed conflict, not only with Malaysia, but also with Britain, Australia and New Zealand (which had defense agreements with Malaysia).

Throughout this period, the Indonesian Communist Party (PKI) grew steadily in strength and influence in Indonesia, much to the unease of the military. The PKI drew international support, first from the Soviet Union, and later from China. In 1965, an abortive coup d'etat gave the armed forces the pretext to wipe out the PKI and its supporters in a bloodbath which resulted in up to one million people being killed. President Sukarno was replaced by General (later, President) Suharto, who, from 1965 to 1998, ruled Indonesia without any real opposition, and ushered in a New Order. Although periodic elections were held, political power was not really contestable. The ruling Golkar Party always won the election, and President Suharto was always re-elected president.

After a stormy period in the 1950s, when pro and anti-Communist forces were locked in a battle for political supremacy, Prime Minister Lee Kuan Yew's People's Action Party (PAP) was swept into power in the Singapore 1959 general election. By 1963, Singapore had joined the Federation of Malaysia. However, before long, irreconcilable political differences between the two parties led to the Malaysian Prime Minister, Tengku Abdul Rahman, making Singapore an offer it could not refuse. This led to the separation of Singapore from the Federation in 1965, and its existence as an independent, sovereign city-state.

Since that time, Singapore has been ruled by the PAP which has won every general election (albeit with a declining share of the vote) without much opposition. Although one or two opposition leaders have been elected to parliament, they have been ineffective in loosening the PAP's grip on power. Prime Minister Lee held office until 1990 when he resigned and became a Senior Minister in the cabinet. His chosen successor, Goh Chok Tong, took his place as Prime Minister. So, for much of its history as an independent country, Singapore has been ruled by one political party, and (for all intents and purposes) by one man.

In the Philippines, a democratic system of government (based on the US Congressional model) was in operation between 1946 and 1972. In the face of a deteriorating economy, widespread corruption, endemic political violence, and mounting challenges to his political power (centred on the popular Senator Benigno Aquino), President Marcos declared martial law on September 23, 1972. This ushered in a long period of authoritarian rule which ended when President Marcos was forced from office in 1986 as a result of a popular uprising.

During the period of martial law, President Marcos (with the support of the armed forces) took over television and radio stations, shut down unfriendly newspapers, suppressed individual freedoms, and dismissed hundreds of thousands of government employees (from civil servants to judges). His lovely wife, Imelda (the one with all those shoes) became increasingly influential in public affairs, while his children were appointed to important positions. The private wealth of the Marcos family grew rapidly as widespread corruption, nepotism, and crony capitalism saw no bounds under President Marcos' authoritarian rule.

East Asia

With the defeat of the nationalist Kuomintang forces led by Generalissimo Chiang Kai Shek in 1949, the Chinese Communist Party led by Mao Zedong took power in mainland China. On October 1, 1999, China celebrated the 50th anniversary of this momentous event. Chairman Mao established a "dictatorship of the proletariat" in China. To many, it was just a dictatorship with Chairman Mao assuming the role of a new emperor (Salisbury 1992: xiii). In spite of the structure of the Chinese Communist Party, and the functions of the various organs of state, Chairman Mao ruled China with almost absolute authority, accountable to no one. According to his physician, like an emperor, Chairman Mao believed only in his infallibility. He could not be wrong, but if wrong decisions were made,it was because the emperor had been deceived or misled by those around him (Li 1994: 296).

Chairman Mao was paranoid about rightists and counter-revolutionaries who he thought were waiting for an opportunity to seize power and reinstate capitalism in China. As a result of this, he undertook frequent purges of party cadres and officials whose loyalty came under suspicion. The most celebrated example of this was during 1966–76, when he unleashed the Red Guards in a bid to consolidate his grip on power even though this meant the death of many innocent people and the sacrifice of a whole generation of young people who were forced to forgo their education and work in the countryside.

With the death of Chairman Mao in 1976, and the implementation of market-oriented economic reforms shortly afterwards, economic liberalisation took place in China as it embraced the free market. However, the Chairman of the Chinese Communist Party still held the reins of political power tightly. Any opposition to the government (real or imagined) was not tolerated and any calls for democratic reforms were (often brutally) suppressed.

The Tiananmen Massacre in 1989 (in which hundreds of innocent protesters were killed) underlined the government's resolve that, although economic freedoms would be tolerated, political freedoms would not be allowed.

Thus, as China enters the 21st century, it is characterised by a vibrant, free-market economic system (albeit with a large state-owned sector), but a totalitarian form of government under which any form of political dissent, and any challenge to government authority, is ruthlessly suppressed.

The other country in Asia that has had an unbroken history of authoritarian (some would say dictatorial) government since the end of the Second World War is North Korea. Under the Great Leader, Kim Il Sung, North Korea was ruled by a totalitarian government for over 40 years. As in similiar Communist regimes in other parts of the world (the former East Germany comes to mind), political dissent was suppressed and any challenge to authority was crushed. After the Great Leader's death in 1994, his son, Kim Jong Il (the Dear Leader) took over the reins of power (after a decent interregnum), and continued the policies of his father. In the late 1990s, North Korea remained the only country (other than Cuba) which has retained the Communist system of central planning, and one of the longest surviving totalitarian states in the world.

AUTHORITARIAN STATES AND ECONOMIC DEVELOPMENT

There is a view that says that strong, authoritarian states are conducive to rapid economic growth and development especially in less developed countries (Fukuyama 1992: 41; Macintyre 1994: 4–6). The obverse of this is the view that democracy (especially, excessive democracy) is inimical to rapid growth and development (Lee 1992: 29).

The reason for this is that strong, authoritarian governments provide political stability, continuity of economic policies, and are able to implement painful economic reforms and other policy decisions quickly and effectively, without endless debate, without being captive to vested interests groups, and without fear of being thrown out of office at the next election (if it is held).

However, strong, authoritarian government, *per se*, is not sufficient to bring rapid economic growth. Many parts of Asia, Africa and Latin America are littered with economies that have been plundered and wrecked by authoritarian governments. What is also needed is a highly-disciplined, competent, efficient and honest public administration which is able to implement government policies without fear or favour. It is the combination of "technocratic economic rationalism with paternalistic authoritarianism" that characterises the high-growth economies of Southeast and East Asia (Fukuyama 1992: 243). Another important ingredient is the quality of the political leadership. In countries in which the quality of leadership is poor, where political leaders are barely educated, or where politicians have to pander to populist sentiments, the quality of decision-making is also likely to be poor (Lee 1998: 331–342).

Highly democratic governments suffer from having to endure endless policy debates, to accommodate various, and competing, interest groups, and a constant need to maximise their re-election prospects. As a result of this, governments in highly democratic less developed countries are unable to assure political or policy stability, decisive action, or independence from vested interest groups.

Proponents of the view that authoritarian states are conducive to rapid economic growth and development often point to the fact that the high-growth economies of Asia have all been ruled by authoritarian governments in their periods of rapid growth. Japan, the Asian NICs, China, Indonesia under President Suharto, and Malaysia under Prime Minister Mahathir are often paraded as the prime exhibits in support of this case. In addition, many of the slow-growth economies of Asia have been ruled by democratic governments. India and the Philippines are often mentioned as illustrations. This view is sometimes reinforced by pointing to the fact that the change from authoritarian to democratic governments in South Korea and Taiwan (in the late 1980s) was followed by increased political instability, greater industrial unrest, and much

slower rates of economic growth. A similar change in Japan in the
late 1980s when the Liberal Democratic Party (which had ruled
the country since the end of the Second World War) was replaced
by a series of weak coalition governments is often cited.

At this point in the debate, Asian values are often wheeled in
to support the case for authoritarian governments being associated
with rapid economic growth. It is argued that Asian values, and
Confucian values in particular, support the rise of authoritarian
states. After all, for thousands of years, the teachings of Confucius
were used by the emperors of China to justify a strong, unified,
central government. A frequent variation on this theme is that
people who adhere to Confucian values do not care much for
democratic freedoms. To them, political stability is more important
and as long as they are free to make money and to accumulate
wealth, they care little for democratic freedoms and are prepared
to tolerate authoritarian governments. It is therefore of little
surprise that many of the high-growth economies of Southeast and
East Asia are in countries which espouse Confucian values and
which are characterised by authoritarian governments (Fukuyama
1992: 241).

Not surprisingly, these views have come under strong criticism.
The rise of popular demands for greater democratic freedoms in the
1990s in Hong Kong SAR, South Korea, Taiwan, and China, are often
cited as a refutation of the view that people in Confucian societies do
not care much for democratic freedoms. In 1998, Martin Lee, the
Hong Kong SAR democracy activist, argued that "the supposed
conflict between democracy and Asian values is a false distinction"
(Lee 1999: ii–iii).

The view that authoritarian governments (combined with
relatively honest and efficient public administrations) are superior
vehicles for delivering economic prosperity has also come under severe
attack. The outbreak of the Asian currency crisis in July 1997 made
that view suddenly unfashionable. However, the counter-attack had
begun earlier.

While it is conceded that democracy does not always lead to
economic growth (the Philippines and India are often cited as prime

examples), it is argued that economic growth often leads to democracy. As people grow more affluent and more educated, and as the problems of economic survival recede in terms of urgency, people begin to put higher priority on the quality of life, and this often leads to demands for greater political freedoms (Economist 1994: 15). By the late 1980s, South Korea and Taiwan had reached this stage of development (Pennar 1993: 26). In addition, when countries reach the higher stages of economic development, innovation and creativity (rather than blind obedience) become increasingly important in the bid to remain internationally competitive. The questioning of authority that this involves inevitably spills over into the realm of politics, and generates demands for greater democratic freedoms (Economist 1991: 18). So, even though authoritarian governments may be more effective in starting and implementing the process of rapid economic growth, their very success eventually undermines their longevity. As an advertisement in the Washington Post declared, "Sooner or later, all tyrannies crumble" (Friedman 1999: 59).

However, even the view that authoritarian governments are more likely to be successful in promoting economic growth has been found wanting. Since economic growth often requires the successful implementation of economic reforms, the question has been recast into one which asks if authoritarian, or democratic, regimes have been more successful in this regard. The available evidence suggests that it is democracies rather than authoritarian states that have been more successful in implementing economic reforms (Economist 1994b: 16–17). In addition, political freedoms appear to reinforce the positive effect that economic freedoms have on economic growth. The reason for this is that democracies guarantee the stability of economic policies that are essential for continued investment, which in turn, drives economic growth (Economist 1994b: 17). Unlike authoritarian governments, democracies are less likely to suffer from sudden, and often diametrically opposite, changes in policy, often at the whim of a dictator (in 1987, the Burmese government, under former general, President Ne Win, suddenly announced, without reason, that the country's 25, 35 and 75 kyat notes would no longer be legal tender and would be replaced by 45 and 90 kyat notes. Overnight, a large proportion of the country's currency in circulation became worthless). It is therefore no accident that most countries in the world with a per capita income of US$15,000 per annum (one of the benchmarks of a developed country), are liberal democracies (Friedman 1999: 144). Even in Asia, authoritarian governments have been gradually replaced by democratic ones as the new millennium dawns (FEER 1999: 94).

CONCLUSION

At the end of the Second World War, many countries in Asia attained political independence from their colonial masters. Although many of these countries started out as liberal democracies, few remained so. Within a few years, military dictatorships or authoritarian civilian governments became entrenched, often under the pretext of saving the nation from imminent disaster. Although some of these countries returned, periodically, to democratic forms of government, they often relapsed into authoritarian ones, as the 1999 *coup d'etat* in Pakistan illustrates. In the meantime, many of the authoritarian states in Southeast and East Asia achieved spectacular rates of economic growth in the latter half of the twentieth century.

This has led some to argue that authoritarian governments (when combined with relatively honest and efficient public administrations), are highly conducive to rapid economic growth and development. Some have even argued that as long as these authoritarian governments delivered rising economic prosperity to their peoples, the latter were uninterested in democratic freedoms. Asian values, which are considered to be different from Western values and the latter's emphasis on democratic freedoms are often invoked to support this view.

These views have come under strong criticism. There is no strong evidence to support the view that authoritarian governments are better at achieving high rates of economic growth than democratic ones. Indeed, the opposite is likely to be the case, since the economic reforms and reallocation of resources that are required to achieve rapid economic growth are more likely to be successfully implemented under democratic regimes. In addition, the policy stability and certainty that democratic governments ensure, encourages investment which drives economic growth. Finally, even if authoritarian governments are better at initiating the process of rapid economic growth, rising affluence over time will eventually undermine their continued existence. As people grow richer and become more educated, they will eventually demand a better quality of life and greater democratic freedoms. Many countries in Asia have already reached this stage and have exchanged their authoritarian governments for democratic ones.

CHAPTER **11**

The Paths Towards Democracy

INTRODUCTION

By the end of the 1980s, many countries in Southeast and East Asia had begun to move towards democratic forms of government. In most cases, rising popular resentment (often triggered off by some social or political crisis) against repressive, authoritarian regimes, led to the latter's demise. In some cases, the abject poverty of the masses jarred so much with the opulent wealth of the few (often gained through widespread corruption), that pressures for economic and social justice could no longer be contained. In other cases, increasing affluence and greater educational attainments, reinforced by modern communications technology, and the adoption of market-oriented economic reforms, contributed towards greater demands for democratic freedoms. In almost all cases, public sentiments were galvanised by courageous individuals who risked life and limb, and often endured years of imprisonment and torture, in order to keep alive their dreams of freedom and democracy.

THE ROLE OF EDUCATION

Education is one of the most potent weapons against authoritarianism. As people become more and more educated, they become less and less willing to do as they are told, to carry out orders from above in blind obedience. This is more so if there is an increasingly large group of people who become equally, or more, educated than their rulers. Authoritarian governments know this, and often try their best to restrict access to education especially higher education. This is why colonial governments provided only rudimentary education in their colonies. Basic numeracy and literacy were all that were required for people to be employed as clerks, peons, servants, and other low-level occupations. They knew that highly educated subjects were likely to be disgruntled subjects, hankering for political independence, and greater democratic freedoms.

In the post-colonial period, many countries in Asia made higher education available to their peoples. The problem for authoritarian governments was then transformed to one in which higher education would be provided (since skilled manpower was needed for economic development), but only in certain fields. The arts, medicine, pure sciences and engineering were encouraged as were some of the harder of the social sciences (for example, economics), but other subjects (the softer social sciences such as political science or sociology) were deemed to be undesirable as they could ignite the flames of political dissent. Even when these subjects were taught in universities, authoritarian governments carefully monitored and controlled what was taught. Anything that smacked of, or could be labelled as, meddling in local politics was swiftly dealt with. Criticism was interpreted as opposition. Those not "for" were considered "against". Invisible boundaries were drawn, beyond which it was hazardous to venture. Universities were reduced to little more than sausage machines.

However, with modern technology (in the form of the Internet, the mobile telephone, and the fax machine), opportunities for travel, satellite transmission of television programmes, and the like became greater and it has become increasingly difficult for governments to limit the spread of knowledge amongst their citizens.

The role of science and technology

As the second half of the twentieth century rolled on, science and technology became more and more important, not only in everyday life, but also for countries that wanted to compete efficiently in the global marketplace. As export-oriented industrialisation became the dominant paradigm of economic development, large numbers of scientists and engineers had to be trained for corporations and governments if a country wanted to become, and remain, an important player in a highly competitive global economy. At the lower rungs of the technological ladder, copying and adapting other people's technologies was all that was required. However, at the higher reaches of the technological ladder, creativity and invention were increasingly important. This, however, requires the questioning of authority, the freedom to express one's views, however heretical, the freedom to obtain information, the courage of going against the grain of conventional wisdom, daring to be different, the willingness to express dissenting views. These attitudes soon spill over into the realm of politics, stimulating an appetite for greater democratic freedoms (Chee 1999: 325). It is no coincidence that countries which excel in science and technology are also those which guarantee basic democratic rights and freedoms. North Korea has not produced any Nobel laureates.

CAPITALISM AND DEMOCRACY

The essence of capitalism is freedom of choice. One of the principal theorems of laissez-faire capitalism is that if consumers are free to choose how to spend their incomes, what products or services they want to purchase, how they spend their time, what occupations they wish to work in, the operation of free markets will result in an efficient allocation of resources which will produce maximum output and welfare for society as a whole (Friedman and Friedman 1980: 27-58). In a free-market economy, this freedom of choice is not limited to the realm of economics. It soon extends into the realm of politics. When people are free to make economic and financial decisions, they will soon demand the freedom to make political decisions. Those who are free to decide what they want to buy or sell, soon want to decide whom they want to rule them. Thus, according to this view, capitalism and democracy are closely linked. The former cannot exist without the latter for any length of time. Sooner or later, capitalism leads to democratic forms of government (Friedman 1962).

There is another link between capitalism and democracy. For markets to work efficiently, economic agents must have information that is as complete as possible in order to make rational decisions. Without accurate information, rational decisions about whether to buy, sell, or invest, cannot be made correctly. Very expensive mistakes are likely if decisions are made based on inaccurate or partial information. Hence, for capitalism to flourish, freedom of information of all kinds is required. However, as explained above, this is inimical to authoritarian states which often want to control, or limit free access to information in order to maintain their monopoly on power (in the former Soviet Union under Stalin, radio sets were made in such a way that they could not be tuned to receive the BBC World Service). Thus, in countries in which a free-market economy is thriving, access to information is usually free. If such countries are ruled by authoritarian governments, their tenure is likely to be more and more uncertain over time. The freedom of information that free markets require to function effectively, will eventually undermine the grip of authoritarian rulers.

GLOBALISATION

These trends were strengthened in the late 1980s when advances in modern communications technology, the collapse of Communism, and the dominance of the capitalist market system, ushered in the age of globalisation. As countries became more and more integrated into the world economy, the demarcations between economics and politics became increasingly blurred, and domestic political issues could not be quarantined within national borders.

In a globalised economy, the imperatives of international finance are likely to reinforce the trends towards democratic forms of government. Democratic governments are more likely to exhibit the flexibility in policy formulation, implementation and response that is required in world economy that is subject to unpredictable shocks. Moreover, the often painful adjustments that need to be made in the wake of these shocks require a legitimacy that authoritarian governments usually lack. People are less willing to do as they are told, less unwilling to question government policies when times are bad and they are hurting. In addition, any changes or improvements that are made are more likely to be widely supported, and therefore more sustainable if they are made under a democratic system of government since the people have had a say in their formulation and adoption. Unlike authoritarian regimes, democratic governments have to be accountable to the people, can be replaced if they do not perform well, encourage the free flow of information, do not stifle criticism, have a free press and an independent judiciary (Friedman 1999: 157–159).

In a global economy, international investment will tend to flow to countries with democratic forms of government. They will be rewarded with higher rates of economic growth, and higher standards of living, as they obtain the resources and technologies from the rest of the world to develop their economies. The pressures exerted by international finance will push countries towards the path of democratisation. Those who prefer to remain authoritarian will be left out of the global economy and out of the economic prosperity that could have been enjoyed. One needs only to think of countries like Myanmar or North Korea, and compare them with Taiwan or Singapore.

POLITICAL DISSIDENCE

The paths to democracy are usually opened up by a few courageous individuals who have refused to remain silent in the face of oppression. These political dissidents have paid a high price, not only in terms of their personal well-being, but also in terms of the harsh treatment meted out to their families and friends. Some have paid the ultimate price for their convictions. They have been the beacons in a sea of darkness, around which people have gathered, and, in some cases, triumphed over despots. From Mohandas Gandhi to Nelson Mandela, from Aung San Suu Kyi to Wei Jingshen, political dissidents have been the light at the end of the political tunnel, those who were brave enough to take the first step in the metaphorical journey of a thousand *li*.

Political dissidents have a number of characteristics in common. They are usually innocent of the alleged crimes for which they have been imprisoned; have a clear sense of right and wrong; an inability to look the other way, to remain silent and avoid becoming involved in the face of injustice and oppression; a burning desire for an improvement in the lives of their fellow citizens and for their country; a stubborn adherence to their beliefs; an inability to compromise on matters of principle; and a strange capacity for forgiveness towards those by whose hands they have unjustly suffered unspeakable hardships.

In 1962, whilst on military duty on one of the islands off the Taiwanese coast, Shih Ming-teh was arrested and charged with plotting to overthrow the Kuomintang Government of Generalissimo Chiang Kai-shek. Although he had, in earlier years, organised and participated in meetings of students during which social and political issues were discussed, Shih denied that these were anything more than discussion groups. However, like many native Taiwanese, he did not hide his dislike for the harsh manner in which mainlanders treated his compatriots. After two years of detention and torture, he was brought before a military tribunal, found guilty, and sentenced to life imprisonment. Following a general amnesty for political prisoners after the death of Chiang Kai-shek in 1975, Shih's sentence was reduced to 15 years. When he was released in 1977, he threw himself in to local politics, supporting and working for non-Kuomintang (*dangwai*) politicians. In 1980, he was arrested again, and spent another 10 years in prison. In 1987, President Chiang Ching-kuo, who succeeded his father, lifted martial law (under pressure from the USA), and offered Shih an amnesty. Shih refused, insisting that amnesty was a pardon for criminals, and that accepting such an offer would be an admission of a guilt that he had consistently denied. In 1990, President Lee Teng-hui (a native Taiwanese who succeeded Chiang Ching-kuo) again offered Shih an amnesty. This time, he accepted, as most of his demands had been met (all other political prisoners had been freed, martial law has been abolished, and the murder and harassment of opposition politicians had been halted). In 1992, Shih was elected to the

Legislative Yuan. His first public act was to forgive the Kuomintang members and ministers in the Yuan for the years of brutal treatment that he had received from their government (Chee 1999: 7–51).

In the Philippines, the political rivalry between Ferdinand Marcos (who was elected President in 1965) and the then Governor of Tarlac province, Benigno Aquino, had begun in the 1960s. The strained political relationship between them intensified when Aquino was subsequently elected to the Senate. Senator Aquino was a painful thorn in the side of President Marcos, exposing the government's covert military operations against East Malaysia (the "Corregidor Affair"), and ridiculing the First Lady Imelda Marcos's grandiose plans to build a cultural centre. By the early 1970s, widespread popular unrest had broken out in the Philippines as mismanagement of the economy led to declining rates of economic growth and spiralling inflation. Violent demonstrations erupted, and bombs went off in public places. In 1972, a staged assassination attempt on the Defence Secretary, Jose Enrile, was the trigger that prompted President Marcos to declare martial law. One of the consequences of this was the arrest and imprisonment of Senator Benigno Aquino, who was later sentenced to death by a tribunal on charges of murder and treason. Under pressure from the USA, the sentence was not carried out. Whilst in prison, Aquino suffered a heart attack and was allowed to leave with his family for the USA to undergo bypass surgery. He stayed on in the USA after recovering from the operation, and took up fellowships at Harvard University and at the Massachusettes Institute of Technology. Meanwhile, in the Philippines, economic and social conditions began to deteriorate, with violent clashes between demonstrators and riot police becoming increasingly commonplace. Bombs started exploding in the Manila CBD. In 1981, under pressure from the USA, President Marcos (now seriously ill with kidney disease) lifted martial law and announced that fresh presidential elections would be held. Encouraged by his supporters, Aquino decided to return to the Philippines in 1983 to contest the presidential elections. He did not get past the tarmac at Manila airport, where he was assassinated as he was leaving his aircraft (Chee 1999: 155–195).

In 1961, after 10 years of being thwarted by political rivals and government officials, Kim Dae Jung was elected to the South Korean National Assembly. Three days later, General Park Chung Hee staged a *coup d'etat*, ushering in a long period of military rule in South Korea. General Park soon discarded his military uniform and got himself elected as President of South Korea, beating Kim Dae Jung for the job in 1971. In 1973, South Korean CIA (KCIA) operatives kidnapped Kim in Tokyo and transported him back to South Korea. It was only the intervention of the US ambassador that saved Kim's life. He was placed under house arrest and jailed for one year on trumped-up charges. Meanwhile, President Park had managed to persuade the National Assembly to declare him president for life. A new consititution was written (the *Yushin* constitution) which denied South Koreans basic democratic rights. Even criticism of the government was regarded as a threat to national security and was punishable by death. Any opposition to the government was put down ruthlessly. In 1974 President Park narrowly escaped an assassination attempt (in which his wife was killed). In 1976, Kim Dae Jung was arrested, along with several others, for demonstrating in Myong Dong cathedral against the government. He was sentenced to five years imprisonment. President Park was assassinated in 1979 by the chief of his own intelligence agency (the KCIA). He was succeeded by General Chun Doo Hwan, who will be remembered as the person who ordered the Kwangju massacre in 1980, in which thousands of student demonstrators and innocent civilians were killed. Kim Dae Jung was arrested and charged for inciting the riots in Kwangju and other parts of the country and for attempting to overthrow the government. He was found guilty and sentenced to death. Under pressure from the USA Japan, and European countries, Kim's sentence was commuted to 20 years' imprisonment. In 1982, he was allowed to leave, with his family, for the USA, where he was to receive treatment for arthritis. He returned to South Korea in 1985 and was promptly placed under house arrest. In 1987, amidst widespread student demonstrations against his regime, President Chun stepped down in favour of his hand-picked successor, General Roh Tae Woo. General Roh freed

Kim Dae Jung and other political prisoners and called new presidential elections which he duly won. In 1992, another political dissident, Kim Yong Sam was elected president (instead of Kim Dae Jung) after cutting a deal with President Roh. President Kim Yong Sam's tenure was marred by rampant corruption. His greatest act was to order the arrest of his two predecessors, Presidents Chun Doo Hwan and Roh Tae Woo. This, however, could not secure his political future. In 1998, Kim Dae Jung was elected president of South Korea. After more than 30 years in the political wilderness, the political dissident was elected to the highest office in the land (Chee 1999: 197–240).

Despots seldom relinquish their grip on power voluntarily. The trappings and privileges of power, once enjoyed, are difficult to forego without a fight. In the battle between the Davids and Goliaths of this world, it is the Goliaths who often win because it is they who have the means of coercion at their disposal to neutralise their opponents and render them ineffective. This is why, political dissidents, on their own, can seldom bring about the democratic changes for which they have struggled.

There are countries in which political dissidents have languished in jails for years on end, almost forgotten by all except their loved ones, without ever achieving their dreams of a more democratic society. In such cases, the catalysts that are required to transform their dreams into reality are usually absent. There is insufficient movement in the snow to cause an avalanche. Often, it is some social or political crisis that galvanises popular support around political dissidents, that sweeps away autocratic rulers in the same way that an avalanche, starting from small beginnings, sweeps away everything in its path.

In the case of Taiwan, changes in geopolitics made it increasingly necessary for the Taiwanese Kuomintang government to succumb to pressure from the USA to implement democratic reforms. The *détente* between the USA and the Peoples' Republic of China in the early 1970s, the subsequent admission of China to the United Nations, and its replacement of Taiwan on the Security Council, and the increasing diplomatic isolation of

Taiwan in world affairs, all made it necessary for the Kuomintang government to relax its monopoly on political power. Thus, although Shih Ming-teh and other political dissidents did play an important role in Taiwan's movement towards democracy by bringing the brutal and repressive policies of the Kuomintang government to international attention, larger geopolitical forces eventually brought about Taiwan's transformation from authoritarianism to democracy.

In the Philippines, it was the assassination of Senator Benigno Aquino in 1983 that sparked off widespread social unrest for the removal of President Marcos. Hundreds of thousands of people stood in the paths of tanks and guns. However, it was only after the Defense Secretary, Jose Enrile, and Vice-Chief of Staff, General Fidel Ramos, deserted President Marcos and sided with the people, that the tide turned against the president. The power of the people, backed by the moral authority of the Catholic church, and the support of the factions of the armed forces loyal to Enrile and Ramos, drove President Marcos from Malacanang Palace into exile in the USA.

In South Korea, years of brutality under military dictatorships (disguised as civilian governments), combined with widespread corruption and the concentration of wealth, generated increasing social and political unrest amongst the population at large. Rapid economic growth and rising incomes during much of the 1960s, 1970s, and 1980s, blunted the edge of widespread dissatisfaction amongst the people. By the late 1980s, however, the South Korean economic miracle had begun to lose its brilliance as world economic conditions began to deteriorate. In the late 1980s, under increasing pressure from the USA and other countries, President Chun Doo Hwan relaxed many of the restrictions that had been placed on individual freedoms. This only allowed an increase in the tide of social and industrial unrest in the country, which eventually swept away the long legacy of authoritarian rule in South Korea and eventually installed Kim Dae Jung in the Presidential Blue House.

THE EMERGENCE OF DEMOCRATIC GOVERNMENTS

In the middle of the 1980s, "people power" in the Philippines forced President Marcos (who had imposed martial law in the 1970s) from office, and elected Corazon Aquino (wife of the murdered Benigno "Ninoy" Aquino) as President of the republic. By the late 1980s, South Korea and Taiwan shifted from military dictatorships to civilian governments. Although in South Korea, former generals attempted to hold on to power by just discarding their uniforms and wearing business suits, by the early 1990s, this was no longer tolerated by the South Korean people who elected, as president, a former political dissident, Kim Yong Sam in 1992, and another former political dissident, Kim Dae Jung, in 1998. The outbreak of the Asian currency crisis in the middle of 1997 also led to the installation of democratically-elected governments, first in Thailand, and then in Indonesia. In November 1997, the then Prime Minister of Thailand, former general Chavalit Yongchaiyud resigned under popular pressure, and was replaced by Chuan Leekpai. In May 1998, widespread riots on the streets of Jakarta forced the resignation of President Suharto, who was replaced by his vice-president, Dr B. J. Habibe. In August 1999, the first free elections in Indonesia since the 1950s were held. This later resulted in the election of President Abdurrahman Wahid in October 1999. Within the relatively short space of about 15 years, authoritarian government were swept aside in several Southeast and East Asian countries.

Nevertheless, several authoritarian governments remain in Southeast and East Asia. Myanmar and China, are perhaps, the best examples, but several other countries in Southeast Asia (especially amongst the former Indo-Chinese states) also come to mind. However, even those governments in Asia that have remained authoritarian, are arguably less so than they were in previous decades. Moreover, as the "changing of the guard" inevitably occurs in these countries, and a new generation of political leaders takes over, the rising tide of popular demands for greater democratic freedoms may yet sweep over their peoples.

CONCLUSION

By the late 1980s, many countries in Southeast and East Asia had begun to implement democratic reforms, often ending years of authoritarian government or military rule and shifting to elected governments. Rapid economic growth, rising affluence, increasing educational attainments, and changes in modern communications technology, all worked to undermine and loosen the grip on power which authoritarian rulers had monopolised for years. In some cases, the rapacious or brutal behaviour of some authoritarian governments hastened their demise.

In many countries, political dissidents played an important role in bringing domestic, as well as international, attention to the excesses of authoritarian governments. They became rallying points for popular discontent, which, given the right conditions, unleashed forces which eventually brought down authoritarian governments, and sent despots fleeing into exile.

Not all countries in Asia have followed these trends. Some are still in the grip of authoritarian rulers, or military dictators. However, as Cold War warriors grow old and fade away, a new generation of leaders will take their place, and hopefully, be more willing to grant their people the democratic freedoms for which they yearn.

12

The War on Terror

INTRODUCTION

The world changed irrevocably on September 11, 2001. On that day, a group of terrorists hijacked and deliberately crashed two commercial aircraft into the twin towers of the World Trade Centre in New York. Another aircraft was commandeered and steered into the Pentagon building in Washington. A fourth aircraft was allegedly headed for the White House, but crashed in Pennsylvania before it could reach its target. Many innocent lives were lost as a result of these terrorist attacks carried out on American soil.

These acts of barbarism galvanised the American government into launching a war on terror which was to have far-reaching consequences for the world, not least in Asia.

The world changed forever after "911" (as September 11, 2001, is now commonly referred to). The most powerful nation on earth could not protect itself from devastating terrorist attacks. Fear swept through the rest of the world as countries took whatever measures they could to minimise the likelihood of them being the next targets of terrorism. Large amounts of resources and energies were diverted to this task. The consequences for the world, and for Asia, were far-reaching.

SEPTEMBER 11, 2001

On September 11, 2001, a group of terrorists linked to the Al-Qaeda ("The Base") network, headed by Osama bin Laden, hijacked four commercial aircraft in the United States. Two of these aircraft were deliberately crashed into the twin towers of the World Trade Centre in New York, killing some 3,000 people and bringing the two massive towers of the Trade Centre crashing to the ground. A third aircraft was deliberately crashed into the Pentagon building, while a fourth, allegedly on its way to the White House, crashed in Pennsylvania. Many people died as a result.

In the United States, and later in other countries, people began to avoid travelling by air. The impact on the world airline industry was devastating. Several large airlines in the US and elsewhere filed for bankruptcy. Increased security at airports and on aircraft did not allay the fears that were engendered by 911. Public confidence was at an all-time low.

THE WAR ON TERROR

The 911 attacks galvanised the American government into action. The attacks, the first large-scale terrorist attacks to be perpetrated on American soil, were seen as an act of war. President George W. Bush declared a "war on terror", naming Iraq, Iran and North Korea as an "axis of evil", and promising to pursue terrorists as well as governments that harboured and supported them.

WAR IN AFGHANISTAN

The first country on which the Americans trained their sights was Afghanistan. There, the ultra-fundamentalist Muslim Taliban government (made up mainly of ethnic Pashtuns) had not only harboured, but also had close contact with Osama bin Laden, leader of the Al-Qaeda terrorist network. They even allowed several Al-Qaeda training camps to be established, where many of the 911 bombers had trained. Repeated calls by the US government for the Taliban to deliver Osama bin Laden to them, in order to charge him with the 911 bombings, fell on deaf ears. Taliban leaders protested that they did not know where Osama bin Laden was hiding, and even suggested that he had left Afghanistan. The Americans were not impressed, and soon put together a coalition of forces in order to invade Afghanistan.

The fall of the Taliban

In October, 2001, American and British forces, supported by a coalition of other Western countries, invaded Afghanistan after a brief, but intense aerial bombardment. On the ground, coalition forces joined with the Northern Alliance (a group of largely non-Pashtun Afghans opposed to the Taliban), and drove the Taliban government from power in December 2001.

After the fall of the Taliban government, coalition forces mounted a concerted effort to locate Osama bin Laden and his lieutenants. This proved to be unsuccessful. It is widely believed that Osama bin Laden and his followers, as well as many Taliban leaders (led by their spiritual head, Mullah Omar) had escaped into neighbouring Pakistan, whose western provinces were also inhabited, not only by Muslims, but also by Pashtuns, who supported both the Taliban as well as Osama bin Laden. Although several prominent Al-Qaeda members had been captured, as late as March 2003, Osama bin Laden had still not been apprehended.

Impact on Pakistan

The fall of the Taliban in Afghanistan had far-reaching consequences for neighbouring Pakistan. Under US pressure, the military government of Pakistan, under General Musharraf (who seized power in a bloodless *coup d'etat* in October 1999 and declared himself President in 2001), had supported the invasion of Afghanistan by coalition forces. This had provoked the anger of many Pakistanis, especially those in the western provinces (later governed by fundamentalist Muslim political parties after state elections were held in late 2002) bordering Afghanistan. This created the potential for political and social unrest in Pakistan, a situation that was prevented only by the stringent measures imposed by the military government, determined to put the lid on such developments.

The shift to Southeast Asia

Although the Al-Qaeda terrorist network had been spreading its influence and activities in Southeast Asia before the fall of the

Taliban government, it is widely believed by terrorism experts that, after the coalition victory in Afghanistan in December 2001, Al-Qaeda shifted its operations to Southeast Asia.

This appeared to be a natural development. Southeast Asia contains the world's largest Muslim country (Indonesia), as well as other countries with large Muslim populations (Malaysia, Philippines, Thailand). After the fall of the Suharto regime (which suppressed these groups), many of these groups resurfaced and reorganised themselves in Indonesia. Some young Muslim men from these countries had travelled to Afghanistan to be trained in the Al-Qaeda camps, and to take part in the *jihad* during the Russian occupation of that country. There, they fell under the spell of Osama bin Laden. Some Southeast Asian countries therefore provided fertile ground for Al-Qaeda to sink its roots.

In Southeast Asia, Al-Qaeda operated mainly through sympathetic radical Muslim organisations, many of which it funded and trained.

In Indonesia, Al-Qaeda had close links with the Laskar Jihad ("Holy War Warriors", LJ) and the Majelis Mujahidin Indonesia ("Indonesian Mujahidin Council", MMI). The LJ were largely responsible for the sectarian violence in the Moluccas islands, in which many people were murdered. The military wing of the MMI, the Laskar Jundullah ("Army of Allah", LJH), gained notoriety by attacking nightclubs in Jakarta, and by seeking out Americans in hotels in the capital and elsewhere, threatening them with violence if they did not leave the country immediately (Ministry of Home Affairs 2003: 5, 8).

The group with perhaps the most important links with Al-Qaeda is Jemaah Islamiyah ("Islamic Community", JI). This organisation began as the Darul Islam ("House of Islam", DI) before the Second World War. After Indonesia was granted independence in 1949 by the Dutch, the DI continued to pursue its goal of an Islamic state in Indonesia, something which the government of President Sukarno eschewed. In the mid-1980s, several leaders of the DI fled to Malaysia in order to escape arrest by the Suharto government. There they regrouped, expanded their activities to other countries (notably Singapore), and renamed themselves Jemaah Islamiyah.

The founder of the JI, the late Abdullah Sungkar, had visited Afghanistan in the 1980s, where he forged close links with Al-Qaeda and arranged for many JI members to be trained. When he died in 1999, the Indonesian cleric, Abu Bakar Bashir, took over as leader of the JI.

The JI has, as its main objective, the creation of an Islamic state in Southeast Asia. This would include Indonesia, Malaysia, Mindanao, Singapore and Brunei. It has an economic wing which helps to fund its activities. In 1999, the JI formed a regional network with other radical Muslim groups called the Rabitatul Mujahadin ("Mujahadin Coalition", RM) in order to foster closer co-operation, share resources, and carry out joint operations. In 2000, the RM was responsible for the bomb attack on the Philippine embassy in Jakarta. The JI itself was responsible for the bomb attacks on several churches in Indonesia, and on the Light Railway train in Manila in December of that year (Ministry of Home Affairs 2003: 6–7). Al-Qaeda also operates through other radical Muslim groups in other Southeast Asian countries.

In Malaysia, it is closely linked to the Kumpulan Militan Malaysia ("Militant Group of Malaysia", KMM) whose aim is to establish an Islamic state in that country. The JI also has close links with the KMM. Several of the 911 bombers visited Malaysia in 2000 under the aegis of the JI in Malaysia. These two groups also assisted each other in the procurement of supplies for their terrorist activities (Ministry of Home Affairs 2003: 3, 8).

In the Philippines, Al-Qaeda's links are with the Moro Islamic Liberation Front (MILF) and the Abu Sayyaf Group (ASG). The latter gained notoriety by carrying out a series of kidnappings of foreign tourists both in the Philippines, and in nearby Malaysian island resorts. The MILF also has close links with the JI, providing the latter with training facilities at its Camp Abu Bakar (Ministry of Home Affairs 2003: 3, 8).

The Jemaah Islamiyah in Singapore

In Singapore, the JI was led by a charismatic religious teacher called Ibrahim Maidin. He had visited Afghanistan in the early 1990s, where he fell under the spell of the Taliban and Osama bin Laden. From the late 1990s, the Singapore JI planned several terrorist attacks in Singapore. Targets included the water pipes running from Malaysia to Singapore (which carry 40% of Singapore's water supply), Changi International Airport, the Ministry of Defence headquarters at Bukit Gombak, oil refineries on Jurong island, Mass Rapid Transit railway stations and its Operations Control Centre, and the Ministry of Education headquarters. There were also plans to bomb the US, UK, Australian and Israeli embassies in Singapore. Video tapes of the JI's surveillance of some of these targets were found in Afghanistan by the Americans. Some of these plans were never carried out (for reasons unknown), others were thwarted by the arrest of 15 people (mostly JI members, including Ibrahim Maidin) in December 2001, and a further 21 persons (the majority of whom were JI members) in August 2002. This severely disrupted, but did not eliminate, the threat of terrorist attacks in Singapore by the JI (Ministry of Home Affairs 2003: 2, 10–14).

The Bali bombings

The shift of terrorist activity from the Middle East to Southeast Asia was given dramatic poignancy when on October 12, 2002, three bombs were set off in, or near, nightclubs on the tourist island of Bali. These killed some 300 people, many of whom were Australians on holiday.

These bombings were widely attributed to the JI. Subsequent arrests and interrogations of some of the alleged perpetrators, and of the JI's leader, Abu Bakar Bashir, appear to support this view.

After the Bali bombings, there could no longer be any doubt that the terrorists' theatre of war had shifted to Southeast Asia.

THE WAR ON IRAQ

With the Taliban ousted from Afghanistan and the country loosely in the hands of the pro-Western government of Mohamed Karzai, the Americans turned their attention to Iraq. There, the government of Saddam Hussein had long been suspected of acquiring weapons of mass destruction (WMD), a term used to include nuclear, biological and chemical weapons. In any case, the new US President, George W. Bush, had some old scores to settle with Saddam Hussein, some unfinished business that his father, President George Bush Senior, had left after the end of the first Gulf War in 1991. The Americans had also named Iraq as one component of the "axis of evil", claiming that it had close links with terrorist organisations such as Al-Qaeda, and fearing that if Iraq was not disarmed, some WMD might get into the hands of these terrorist organisations.

The Americans (supported by their close allies, the UK and Australia) took the view that if Iraq did not disarm voluntarily, it would be disarmed by the use of force. In preparation for this, the US and its allies started deploying their forces to the Middle East, in readiness for war.

Under international pressure, the US and its "coalition of the willing" were forced to seek a mandate from the UN Security Council. This they did, obtaining a unanimous vote for Resolution 1441, under which Iraq was required to divest itself of its WMD under the aegis of UN arms inspectors.

The painstaking work of the UN arms inspectors proved to be slow and time-consuming. Under increasing pressure, the Iraqi regime grudgingly increased its co-operation with the arms inspectors. At the same time, the US dismissed these as mere token measures, designed to prolong the inspection process.

In mid-March 2003, the US and UK announced that they would table a new resolution in the UN Security Council, under which force would be sanctioned if the Iraqi government failed to comply with UN demands to disarm. Meanwhile, more and more members of the Security Council, some with the right of veto, began to openly disagree with the US position.

At the end of March 2003, the USA (in coalition with the UK and Australia) decided not to proceed with obtaining a new UN resolution, and launched a war on Iraq. The Iraqi regime of Saddam Hussein, despite much bravado, was defeated in 21 days, after an intense and massive aerial bombardment, followed by a ground attack. The Iraqi people paid a heavy price in death and misery for the removal of Saddam Hussein's brutal dictatorship.

Impact on oil prices

One important consequence of the war on Iraq would be a rise in world oil prices. In the 1991 Gulf War, crude oil prices rose briefly to US$38 per barrel, before falling, once it was clear that coalition forces would win the war. In March 2003, even before war had begun, crude oil prices had reached these high levels. The outbreak of war would drive these prices even higher.

Since, with few exceptions, most countries are net oil importers, the consequences of a steep rise in the price of oil would have devastating consequences for their economies. The costs of production, transport and other raw materials would rise, leading possibly to a worldwide recession. The prospect of an imminent war had already sent stock markets around the world tumbling dangerously, as investors dumped shares in favour of gold.

Increased terrorist attacks

Another likely consequence of the war on Iraq is increased terrorist attacks on Western (mainly US) targets around the world. Neither the US, the UK nor the Australian government has been successful in convincing the Muslim world that the war on terrorism (and on Iraq) is not a war on Muslims or on Islam. On the other hand, it has been relatively easy for radical Muslim leaders to convice their followers that the opposite is, indeed, the case, that the war on terror is an attack on Islam. Even highly educated, and moderate, Muslim leaders have been unable, or unwilling, to distinguish between a war on terrorists *qua* terrorists, from a war on Muslims and on Islam.

One of the aftermaths of the war on Iraq is therefore likely to be increased international terrorism and all that that entails.

One example will suffice to underline the point. Already, as a consequence of the 911 terrorist attacks, people have been more reluctant to fly. The world airline industry has been reeling as a result of a significant reduction in passengers. Some major airlines have declared bankruptcy. In 2002, the world airline industry lost US$13 billion (up from the US$18 billion it lost in 2001). Not only has demand for air travel fallen after the 911 terrorist attacks, but costs have also risen, as increased security measures at airports and on aircraft have had to be implemented, and higher insurance costs (which rose by five times) have had to be outlaid. In 2003, the number of airline passengers (some 1.6 billion each year) declined by 2.5% (The Straits Times 2003b: 18).

In early April 2003, the world airline industry was dealt another body blow. The outbreak of a deadly, infectious pneumonia called SARS (Severe Acute Respiratory Syndrome) in China spread quickly to Hong Kong SAR, Vietnam and Singapore. Soon, over 20 countries (including Canada, USA, UK, Germany and France) were reporting cases. Without any cure or treatment, panic swept the infected countries as the number of cases exceeded 3,000, and deaths climbed to over 150. SARS forced many airlines to curtail their operations, as people stayed at home. Its impact on the world airline industry could be more devastating than the war on terror, or the war in Iraq.

THE IMPACT ON ASIA

The impact of the war on terrorism, and the war on Iraq, would be crippling for Asia, especially for Southeast Asia. Costs would rise, revenues would fall, trade and investment would decline, tourism would dry up, and severe economic recession would set in. Some countries in the region have already felt these effects.

Increased security and defence

The rise in costs would be caused not only by higher oil prices (as explained above), but also by increased costs of security and defence, as countries try to protect themselves from increased terrorist attacks. Already the budgets for defence, intelligence, military personnel, and new equipment have risen in several countries. This is likely to continue. The war on terror will be a long war.

Less tourism

Another consequence of the war on terror has been a severe decline in tourism in many Southeast Asian countries. After the Bail bombings, tourists fled the region, vowing never to return. Even Singapore, which boasts of being a relatively safe tourist destination, suffered from the steep decline in tourism. In late 2002, a series of bomb scares emptied Singapore's major tourist spots. Boat Quay, Clarke Quay, and Holland Village were virtually deserted as a result. Even on busy Orchard Road, few European tourists can be seen wandering around, compared to a few years ago.

Less foreign investment

The war on terror has also reduced foreign direct investment in Southeast Asia. Companies, especially US multinationals, are reluctant to invest in Southeast Asia for fear of becoming terrorist targets.

In November 2002, it was reported that the flow of Foreign Direct Investment (FDI) into the Malaysian manufacturing sector had been so low that the Malaysian government had decided to stop releasing monthly figures! In the first six months of 2002, Malaysia attracted only RM2.2 billion of FDI, compared to RM18.8 for the whole of 2001. On average, Malaysia usually attracts RM15 billion of FDI (The Straits Times 2002b: 4). A similar situation has occurred in Indonesia, where in 2002, FDI pledges plunged by 35% compared to the previous year. FDI approvals totalled only US$9.4 billion in 2002, compared to US$15.06 in 2001 (The Straits Times 2003a: A1).

Lower growth in the West

Rising costs and declining consumer confidence are also likely to lower rates of economic growth in the US as well as in other Western countries. This is likely to reduce the demand for the exports of many Southeast Asian countries.

Reduced economic growth in the USA has already been felt in some Southeast Asian countries that depend on the USA for large shares of the exports. Exports have fallen, economic growth rates have diminished, and unemployment has risen, significantly.

Slower economic growth

In many Southeast Asian countries, the war on terror has meant slower rates of economic growth. The war on Iraq will only exacerbate this. For 2003, the rate of economic growth of the Singapore economy is expected to be in the 0.5% to 1.5% range. Unemployment is expected to reach 5.5% (the highest rate in 15 years), and some 80,000 people are expected to become unemployed (The Straits Times 2003c: 5). In most cities in Southeast Asia, rents for office space in the Central Business District (CBD) fell by about 30% in the 12 months to September 2002 (The Straits Times 2002c: 6).

In 2001, Taiwan registered a negative rate of economic growth for the first time in 50 years. The rate of unemployment climbed to more than 5% as the country reeled from the effects of lower exports and a deep recession. In October 2002, some 9,000 people rushed to get application forms for 370 cleaning jobs (The Straits Times 2002d: A5).

The prospects of much slower economic growth, and the significant decline in business as well as consumer confidence, are reflected in the stock market indexes for Southeast Asian countries. Figure 12.1 shows the stock market indexes for the ASEAN countries. There was a sharp drop in stock market prices following the September 2001 terrorist attacks in the USA. Prices recovered from October to December, when the fall of the Taliban government in Afghanistan appeared to signal that the war on terror was being won. They continued to rise until May 2002, and began to fall steadily as negative consequences of the war on terror began to have an economic effect, and a possible war on Iraq deepened negative investor and consumer sentiments. By March 2003, the Philippines had lost 40% of the value of its stock market, compared to January 2001. In Malaysia and Indonesia, stock markets did not lose any value when compared to January 2001. Nevertheless, when compared to their previous peak in May 2002, they had lost between 20% and 40% of their value.

A similar picture can be seen in Figure 12.2, which shows the stock market indexes for the Asian NICs. Again, there was a pronounced drop in stock market prices following the September 2001 terrorist attacks in the USA. Prices recovered from October 2001 until May 2002, after which they fell steadily as investor and consumer sentiment began to erode significantly. By March 2003, Singapore and Hong Kong had lost approximately 40% of the value of their stock markets, and Taiwan about 20%, compared to their value in January 2001.

FIGURE 12.1: ASEAN COUNTRIES' STOCK MARKET INDEXES (JAN 2001=100)

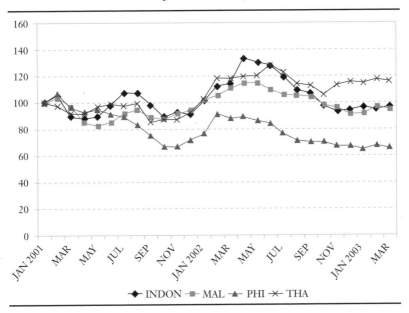

Source: Individual country data

**FIGURE 12.2: ASIAN NICS' STOCK MARKET INDEXES
(JAN 2001=100)**

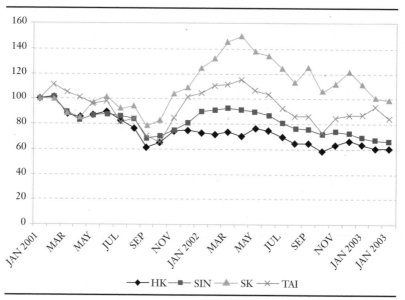

Source: Individual country data

CONCLUSION

Increased expenditures

The war on terror has had, and will continue to have, devastating effects on Asian countries, especially those in Southeast Asia, since the latter depend heavily on the USA for their exports.

Increased expenditures, as a result of beefing up security, increasing intelligence activities, and purchasing new technology to counter terrorism, will have to be incurred, even though revenues are likely to fall significantly. The significant increase in costs is likely to impair international competitiveness, and result in reduced rates of economic growth.

Lower economic growth

Rising costs and slower rates of economic growth in the USA and other Western countries are also likely to reduce foreign investment in many Southeast Asian countries, and dampen their exports. Tourism will also decline as a consequence. Unemployment will rise. As mentioned above, some of these effects are already apparent in many Southeast Asian countries.

The war on terror has therefore had significant negative impacts on many Southeast Asian countries, and will continue to do so for years to come. The outbreak of SARS is likely to intensify these negative impacts.

Even before the 911 terrorist attacks, many countries in Southeast Asia were experiencing declining growth rates as a result of increased competition and rising costs. The war on terror has accelerated these trends.

The halcyon days of high growth and rapidly increasing prosperity in many Southeast Asian countries, from the mid-1960s to the mid-1990s, are now a rapidly fading memory. The short-lived Asian currency crisis of 1998 put a severe dent in the economic prospects of these countries. Even after such a rude shock, many countries in Southeast Asia were starting to recover rapidly, and hoped, within a few years, to regain their stature as economic powerhouses. The war on terror has put an end to these hopes, at least in the short to medium term.

The world will never be the same after September 11, 2001. That day will long be remembered as one of the critical turning points in history. As a result of it, the world has changed in ways that are impossible to fully appreciate at this point in time. What is certain is that life in a post-911 world is going to be more dangerous, more anxious, and less secure, for a long time to come.

CHAPTER **13**

Conclusion

Since the end of the Second World War, the countries of South, Southeast and East Asia have experienced a number of important changes in their economic, social and political structures. Some have been transformed from poor, underdeveloped, agricultural countries to rich, developed, affluent societies, all in the span of less than half a century. Others are still at the beginning stages of this transformation.

Perhaps the most important changes have occurred in the realm of economics. Most, if not all, countries have experienced the shift from a predominantly agricultural economic structure to one that is concentrated on manufacturing activities. In this process, many have been aided by the introduction of new technology in agriculture which has increased productivity and released resources for industrial development. Many countries have also made the shift from import-substitution to export-oriented industrialisation, and have become major world producers and exporters of a number of manufactured goods (of which electronic products are the best known). Although pockets of protection still exist (even in the most export-oriented countries), export-oriented industrialisation is now the dominant development strategy in most Asian countries. This has been accompanied by a shift toward market-oriented economic policies in many Asian countries (including Communist ones, which have largely abandoned central-planning). By the end of the twentieth century, many Asian countries had become highly integrated into the world economy, as globalisation established itself as the dominant system in world affairs. These changes have resulted in rapid economic growth, and rising standards of living in many of the countries in Asia. They have also resulted in economic volatility and financial crises, the most important of the latter being the outbreak of the Asian currency crisis in 1997.

Important social changes have also taken place in many Asian countries. One important change which has had significant consequences is declining fertility. Another is the rapid expansion of educational opportunities especially for women. These have led to important changes in the status and role of women, to the nature of the family unit, and to patterns of marriage and divorce in many Asian countries. While some countries have experienced these changes to a greater extent than others, none has been able to insulate itself completely from these trends.

In terms of politics, many Asian countries, on (or shortly after) gaining independence from their former colonial masters, descended into authoritarian forms of government (often characterised by military dictatorships). While some of these have survived to this day, by the end of the century, many had changed to more democratic forms of government. Even those which have not, are more democratic now than they were several decades ago. In this sense, the trend toward increasing democratisation has been irresistible.

One of the greatest challenges facing Asian countries as they enter the 21st century is accelerating globalisation, spurred on by rapid advances in communications technology. On the one hand, future economic growth and prosperity will depend on how well they integrate with, and become a part of, the global economy in all its manifestations. As Asian countries become more and more integrated with the global economy, they are likely to become recipients of increasingly inflows of foreign capital and technology. These are likely to enable them to accelerate their rates of economic growth and development. On the other hand, increasing globalisation is likely to heighten internal tensions, erode traditional cultures, and generate a backlash against increasing internationalisation. The operation of market forces is likely to increase income inequalities, as the younger, more educated and more skilled benefit more from globalisation than the older, less educated and less skilled. Increasing globalisation is likely to mean, not only higher growth and higher incomes, but also greater volatility (as the Asian currency crisis painfully demonstrated). The "homogenising" effect of globalisation (Friedman 1999: 221) will also tend to threaten traditional cultures, some to the point of near extinction. How the countries of Asia manage this tension between "The Lexus and the olive tree" (Friedmann 1999: 378) will determine whether they remain stuck in the twentieth century or advance with confidence into the next.

In early 2003, the events of September 11, 2001, and their aftermath, caused widespread pessimism about the prospects for the world and the global economy. The war on terrorism, and the rapid spread of SARS, has deepened the negative sentiments of both consumers and investors. The world economy appears to be on the edge of an abyss. For Asian countries, these developments could not have come at a worse time. Just as they appeared to be emerging from the recession following the Asian currency crisis, the downturn in the world economy following the events of September 11, 2001 and the SARS outbreak have cast a pall of gloom over their economic prospects. If, as most observers expect, the war on terror is long and protracted, and if, in addition, SARS is not contained quickly, many Asian countries are unlikely to experience rapid economic growth and development again for a long time to come.

Bibliography

Amaha E 1999, "Blazing a trail", *Far Eastern Economic Review*, July 1, pp. 34-36

Anderson H K, Hill M A and Butler J S 1987, "Age at marriage in Malaysia: a hazard model of marriage timing", *Journal of Development Economics*, Vol 26 No 2, August, pp. 223-234

Ashbrook Jr A G 1975, "China: an economic overview, *1975*", in *Joint Economic Committee Congress of the United States, China: a Reassessment of the Economy* (Washington: US Government Printing Office)

Asian Development Bank 1997, *Emerging Asia: Changes and Challenges* (Manila: Asian Development Bank)

Baker R 1987, "Little emperors' born of a one-child policy", *Far Eastern Economic Review*, July 16, pp. 43-44

Balakrishnan N 1989a, "The state as cupid: a bureaucratic lonely heart's club plans romance", *Far Eastern Economic Review*, August 31, p. 38

Balakrishnan N 1989b, "Battle of the sexes: women grab opportunities presented by economic growth and labour shortage", *Far Eastern Economic Review*, August 31, pp. 34-35

Balakrishnan N 1991, "Single-minded: census fails to allay concern over marriage patterns", *Far Eastern Economic Review*, June 20, p. 17

Blyn G 1983, "The Green Revolution revisited", *Economic Development and Cultural Change*, Vol 31, July, pp. 505-25

Booth A 1998, *The Indonesian Economy in the Nineteenth and Twentieth Centuries* (London: Macmillan)

Bowonder B 1981, "The myth and reality of high-yielding varieties in Indian agriculture", *Development and Change*, Vol 12, pp. 293-313

Cameron L 1999, "Indonesia's social crisis", *Far Eastern Economic Review*, July 8, p. 24

Chee S J 1998, *To be Free: Stories from Asia's Struggle against Oppression* (Melbourne: Monash Asia Institute)

Cheng T Y 1982, *The Economy of Hong Kong* (Hong Kong: Far East Publications)

Commonwealth Universities Yearbook 1992 (London: Association of Commonwealth Universities)

Chua C H 2003, "Beijing's $1.2b bill for clear skies", *The Straits Times*, January 9, p. A2

Crispin S W 1999, "Resting on its laurels: Thailand may lose its biggest hi-tech export", *Far Eastern Economic Review*, August 12, p. 45

Crowley J 1976, "Creation of an empire, 1896-1910", in J Livingston, J More and F Oldfather (eds), *The Japan Reader 1: Imperial Japan 1800-1945* (Harmondsworth: Penguin Books), pp. 225-230

Daorueng P 1998, "Sole sisters", *Far Eastern Economic Review*, September 3, pp. 36-37

Delfs R 1990, "Coming of age: World Bank forecasts pension crisis", *Far Eastern Economic Review*, October 25, pp. 17-18

do Rosario L 1992, "Women in a double bind: they are forced to choose between family and career", *Far Eastern Economic Review*, September 24, pp. 40-41

do Rosario L and Fairclough G 1992, "Toilers of the East: newly rich Asian countries act as a magnet for region's workers", *Far Eastern Economic Review*, April 2, pp. 20-21

Dolven B 1998, "Breaking the mould", *Far Eastern Economic Review*, July 23, pp. 47-49

East Asia Analytical Unit 1997, *The New Aseans: Vietnam, Burma, Cambodia and Laos* (Canberra: Department of Foreign Affairs and Trade)

East Asia Analytical Unit 1992, *South China in Transition* (Canberra: Department of Foreign Affairs and Trade)

Economist 1979, "The 35,000 villages that know that growth works", *Economist*, July 14, pp. 48-50

Economist 1990, "Miracle-workers' reward", *Economist*, April 21, pp. 25-26

Economist 1991, "Freedom and prosperity: Yes, they do march together, but sometimes out of step", *Economist*, June 29, pp. 15-18

Economist 1994a, "Chainsaw massacres", *Economist*, January 25, p. 29

Economist 1994b, "Democracy and growth: why voting is good for you", *Economist*, August 27, pp. 15-17

Economist 1995, "For richer, for poorer", *Economist*, March 18, p. S11

Elegant S 1996, "Dying for attention: lacking parents' counsel, kids turn to crime, drugs", *Far Eastern Economic Review*, August 1, pp. 40-41

FEER 1997, "Abduction of women increasing", *Far Eastern Economic Review*, August 14, p. 27

FEER 1999, "Democracy in Asia: not perfect, but Asians are incrementally more free", *Far Eastern Economic Review*, September 9, p. 94

Fairclough G 1996a, "It isn't black and white", *Far Eastern Economic Review*, March 7, pp. 54-57

Fairclough G 1996b, "Gloom town: can a new governor prevent Bangkok from suffocating?" *Far Eastern Economic Review*, June 20, pp. 22-24

Friedman M 1962, *Capitalism and Freedom* (Chicago: University of Chicago Press)

Friedman M and Friedman R 1980, *Free to Choose* (Harmondsworth: Penguin Books)

Friedman T 1999, *The Lexus and the Olive Tree* (New York: HarperCollins)

Forney M 1996, "The workers' state: for many of them, it's bad and getting worse", *Far Eastern Economic Review*, September 12, pp. 68-69

Fukuyama F 1992, *The End of History and the Last Man* (Harmondsworth: Penguin Books)

Garnaut R and Liu G 1992, *Economic Reform and Internationalisation* (Sydney: Allen and Unwin)

Gilley B 1996, "Following the money: China's growth spurt tempts children into jobs", *Far Eastern Economic Review*, May 7, p. 58

Goldstein C and Huus K 1994, "No workers' paradise: labour activists make little headway in Shenzhen", *Far Eastern Economic Review*, June 16, pp. 35-36

Grabowski R 1998, "Taiwan's economic development: an alternative view", *Development and Change*, Vol 9 No 1, January, pp. 53-68

Greider W 1997, *One World Ready Or Not* (London: Penguin Books)

Hahn E 1963, *China Only Yesterday: 1850-1950 A Century of Change* (London: Weidenfeld and Nicolson)

Halliday J and McCormark G 1973, *Japanese Imperialism Today* (Harmondsworth: Penguin Books)

Handley 1988, "Engineering trained workers: Thailand needs proper policies to produce a qualified workforce", *Far Eastern Economic Review*, September 29, 96-97

Hateley L and Tan G 2003, *The Greying of Asia: Causes and Consequences of Rapid Ageing in Asia* (Singapore: Eastern Universities Press)

Hazell P B R and Ramaswamy C 1991, *The Green Revolution Reconsidered: The Impact of High-Yielding Rice Varieties in South Asia* (Baltimore: John Hopkins University Press)

Hiebert M 1995, "A nice girl like you: Singapore Airlines invests heavily in its biggest asset", *Far Eastern Economic Review*, December 7, p. 79

Hiebert M 1996a, "Help wanted: Singapore scans the globe for skilled professionals", *Far Eastern Economic Review*, June 6, p. 67

Hiebert M 1996b, "The cost of high living: Singapore's new laws aid troubled families", *Far Eastern Economic Review*, August 1, p. 42.

Hiebert M 1996c, "Good idea: Singapore wants students with creative bent", *Far Eastern Economic Review*, November 14, pp. 29-30

Herdt R W 1985, "A retrospective view of technological and other changes in Philippine rice farming, *1865-82*", *Economic Development and Cultural Change*, Vol 35 No 2, pp. 329-51

Hill H and Suphalachalasai S 1992, "The myth of export pessimism (even) under the MFA: evidence from Indonesia and Thailand", *Weltwirtschaftliches Archiv*, Vol 128 No 2, pp. 310-29

Ho Samuel P S 1975, "The economic development of colonial Taiwan", *Journal of Asian Studies*, February

Ho Samuel P S 1984, "Colonialism and development: Korea, Taiwan and Kwantung", in R H Myers and M R Peattie (eds), *The Japanese Colonial Empire 1895-1945* (Princeton: Princeton University Press), pp. 347-98

Hsieh D 2002, "120 million and rising", *The Straits Times*, October 8, p. A3

Islam S 1999, "Death and dishonour: feudal code kills women who challenge tradition", *Far Eastern Economic Review*, May 20, pp. 28-29

Jayasankaran S 1997, "Smoke in your eyes: heavy pollution cuts into the quality of life", *Far Eastern Economic Review*, August 14, p. 20

Johanssen S and O Nygren 1991, "The missing girls of China", *Population and Development Review*, Vol 17 No 1, pp. 35-52

Karp J 1995, "Coax, then hoe: India tills the Green Revolution's new frontier", *Far Eastern Economic Review*, November 16, pp. 91-2

Kaye L 1993, "Have and have-nots", *Far Eastern Economic Review*, September 2, p. 46

Kwan W K 2003, "Poor marks for U of Tokyo grads", *The Straits Times*, January 6, p. A3

Lee K Y 1992, "Discipline vs. democracy", *Far Eastern Economic Review*, December 10, p.29

Lee K Y 1998, "How much is a good minister worth?" in F W Han, W Fernandez and S Tan (eds), *Lee Kuan Yew: The Man and His Ideas* (Singapore: Times Editions)

Lee M 1999, "Introduction", in S J Chee (ed), *To be Free: Stories from Asia's Struggle against Oppression* (Melbourne: Monash Asia Institute)

Li Z 1994, *The Private Life of Chairman Mao* (London: Chatto and Windus)

Lim L Y C 1983, "Singapore's success: the myth of the free market economy", *Asian Survey*, Vol 23 No 6, June, pp. 752-64

Long S 2002, "Thinking of marrying later? No, baby, don't", *The Straits Times*, October 26, p. 29

Macintyre A 1994, "Business, government and development: Northeast and Southeast Asian comparisons", in A Macintyre (ed), *Business and Government in Industrialising Asia* (Sydney: Allen and Unwin), pp. 1-28

Mackerras C 1995, *Eastern Asia: An Introductory History* (Melbourne: Longmans)

MacLeod L 1998, "The dying fields: economic pressures have spawned a tragedy in China — women are killing themselves at an alarming rate", *Far Eastern Economic Review*, April 23, pp. 62-63

McClelland D C 1966, "Does education accelerate economic development?" *Economic Development and Cultural Change*, Vol 14 No 3, April, pp. 257-78

Ministry of Home Affairs 2003, *The Jemaah Islamaiya Arrests and the Threat of Terrorism* (Singapore: Ministry of Home Affairs)

Moran S 1988, "Rise in rural birth rates worries planners", *Far Eastern Economic Review*, March 24, pp. 79-80

Nove A 1983, *The Economics of Feasible Socialism* (London: George Allen and Unwin)

Ohmae K 1990, *The Borderless World* (New York: HarperCollins)

Ohmae K 1995, *The End of the Nation State* (London: HarperCollins).

Oshima H T 1986, "The transition from an agricultural to an industrial economy in East Asia", *The Developing Economies*, Vol 34 No 4, July, pp. 783-809

Paauw D and Fei J 1973, *The Transition in Open Dual Economies* (New Haven: Yale University Press)

Ram M 1979, "Green Revolution on trial", *Far Eastern Economic Review*, August 24

Rhodes B 1993, "Service without a smile: many Filipino workers abroad are abused by their employers", *Far Eastern Economic Review*, November 4, pp. 54-55

Rolston S and Cason S 1996, "Dressed for marital success", *Amida*, April, p. 12

Salisbury H E 1992, *The New Emperors: Mao and Deng* (New York: HarperCollins)

Saw S H 1999, *The Population of Singapore* (Singapore: Institute of Southeast Asian Studies)

Saywell T 1998, "Staying alert: for foreign firms in China, worker safety requires vigilance", *Far Eastern Economic Review*, January 29, pp. 46-48

Scanner 1998, "1997 GCE O Level results: above expectations!" *Scanner*, Vol 14 No 1, June-July, p. 1

Scott M 1989, "Brave new world: the lives of Malaysian, especially Malay, women transformed by factory work", *Far Eastern Economic Review*, December 21, pp. 32-34

Sender H 1999, "Can Asia keep it up?" *Far Eastern Economic Review*, July 8, pp. 30-32

Silverman G 1996, "Vital and vulnerable", *Far Eastern Economic Review*, May 23, pp. 60-66

Singapore Census of Population 1990: Houshold and Housing (Singapore: Department of Statistics)

Singapore Census of Population 2000: Demographic Characteristics (Singapore: Department of Statistics)

Soejono I 1976, "Growth and distribution: changes in incomes of paddy farms in Central Java, 1968-74", *Bulletin of Indonesian Economic Studies*, Vol 12 No 2, July, pp. 80-89

Song Jung A 1999, "Attitude adjustment", *Far Eastern Economic Review*, July 1, p. 35

St John R B 1997, "End of the beginning: economic reform in Cambodia, Laos and Vietnam", *Contemporary Southeast Asia*, Vol 19 No 2, September, pp. 172-189

Tan G 1995, *The Newly Industrializing Countries of Asia* (Singapore: Times Academic Press), Second Edition

Tan G 1997, *ASEAN: Economic Development and Co-operation* (Singapore: Times Academic Press)

Tan G 1999, *The End of the Asian Miracle? Tracing Asia's Economic Transformation* (Singapore: Times Academic Press)

Tan G 2000, *The Asian Currency Crisis: Causes, Consequences and Paths to Recovery* (Singapore: Times Academic Press)

The Straits Times 1998, "Alarm as smog covers HK", *The Straits Times*, September 23, p. 17

The Straits Times 2002a, "S. Korean students are tops among the rich nations", *The Straits Times*, November 27, p. A1

The Straits Times 2002b, "Foreign investments in KL 'too low to publish'", *The Straits Times*, November 6, p. 4

The Straits Times 2002c, "Asia-Pac CBD rents seen sliding further", *The Straits Times*, December 6, p. 6

The Straits Times 2002d, "Up 2% down 11%", *The Straits Times*, October 18, p. A5

The Straits Times 2003a, "Sharp dip in pledges for foreign direct investment", *The Straits Times*, January 9, p. A1

The Straits Times 2003b, "World airline industry suffers $23 billion loss", *The Straits Times*, January 9, p. 18

The Straits Times 2003c, "Jobless rate could peak at 5.5% mid-year", *The Straits Times*, January 10, p. 5

Tiglao R and Scott M 1989, "On the down grade: quantity, not quality, characterises Philippine education", *Far Eastern Economic Review*, July 6, p. 38

Tiglao R 1999, "Roots of poverty", *Far Eastern Economic Review*, June 10, pp. 63-65

Tipton F B 1998, *The Rise of Asia: Economics, Society and Politics in Contemporary Asia* (Melbourne: Macmillian)

Tjondronnegoro S M P, Soejono I and Hardjono J 1992, "Rural poverty in Indonesia: Trends, issues, policies", *Asian Development Review*, Vol 10 No 1, pp. 67-90

Vatikiotis M 1992, "Where has all the labour gone?" *Far Eastern Economic Review*, April 16, pp. 46-47

Vatikiotis M 1996, "Family matters: modern day tensions strain Southeast Asia's social fabric", *Far Eastern Economic Review*, August 1, pp. 38-40

United Nations Commission for Asia and the Pacific 1998, *Asia and the Pacific into the Twenty-First Century: Prospects for Social Development* (New York: United Nations)

United Nations Development Programme 1995, *Human Development Report 1995* (New York: Oxford University Press)

Wong S M and Sim C Y 2002, "Single woman? And in your 30s? Oh dear!", *The Straits Times*, September 27, p. H1

World Bank 1987, *World Development Report* (New York: Oxford University Press)

World Bank 1993, *The East Asian Miracle: Economic Growth and Public Policy* (New York: Oxford University Press)

World Bank 2003, *Human Development Report 2003* (New York: Oxford University Press)

Zeng V and Wong S L 1999, "Chinese entrepreneurship, business network and trust", in Lau S K, Lee M K, Wan P S and Wong S L (eds), *Indicators of Social Development: Hong Kong 1997* (The Chinese University of Hong Kong: Hong Kong Institute of Asia-Pacific Studies)

Index